THE SPORT OF COOKING

THE SPORT of COOKING

The Gourmet Guide for Rookies

PAUL B. ABRAMS

CAPITAL BOOKS, INC.
STERLING, VIRGINIA

Capital Books, Inc.
P.O. Box 605
Sterling, Virginia 20172-0605

ISBN 1-892123-21-5 (alk. paper)

LIBRARY OF CONGRESS
CATALOGING-IN-PUBLICATION DATA

Abrams, Paul B.
   The sport of cooking : the gourmet guide for rookies / Paul B. Abrams. — 1 st ed.
      p. cm.
   ISBN 1-892123-21-5 (alk.)
      1. Cookery. I. Title.

   TX651 .A16 2000
   641.5 — dc21   00-030417

Design and composition by Melissa Ehn at
Wilsted & Taylor Publishing Services

Interior photographs courtesy of
Workbook Co/Op Stock, Los Angeles

Printed in Canada on acid-free paper
that meets the American National Standards Institute
Z39-48 Standard.

First Edition

10 9 8 7 6 5 4 3 2 1

CONTENTS

ACKNOWLEDGMENTS

A special thanks to:

NATALIE R. ABRAMS
Wife, Teacher, Friend, and Critic
For her fabulous taste buds and incredible
"sense of table"

GEORGE KRAMER
Fine Wine Importer
For his superb wine selections

KATHLEEN HUGHES
Publisher, Capital Books, Inc.
For her support of this book

INTRODUCTION

This collection of recipes is designed for having *fun* when planning and preparing a meal for family or friends. Almost every ingredient can be found in the local supermarket. And over 90 percent of these recipes can be prepared with a knife, fork, and spoon, using a frying pan or pot.

- **Recipes** are easy to follow, and each one provides the cook with these guidelines:
- **Degree of Difficulty** rates the recipe from "1" for "easy" to "5" for "difficult." Many recipes have a rating of "1," with most in the "2" and "3" categories.
- **Prep Time** and **Cooking Time** illustrates the length of time required to prepare the recipe from start to finish.
- **Coach's Corner** gives tips for preparation and serving.

Recipes will appeal to rookies and pros alike. Be at ease the first time in the kitchen with any of these world-famous dishes. Every recipe has been kitchen-tested by professionals and everyday cooks.

This book blends two national pastimes by bringing sport into the kitchen. You will find these dishes easy to prepare. They will add variety and excitement to your table. You will learn new and enticing ways of fixing familiar dishes and enjoy traveling to some distant lands with your knife and fork.

MENUS

LINEUP SUGGESTIONS

THE SPORT OF COOKING

APPETIZERS

Melon and Parma Ham

Smoked Salmon with
Honey Mustard Sauce

Carpaccio

Shrimp Cocktail

Spareribs

Cheese Toasts with Basil and
Sun-Dried Tomatoes

Bruschetta: Garlic Toasts with
Tomatoes and Basil

MELON AND PARMA HAM

degree of difficulty: 1
prep time: 5 minutes

Start your meal with a ride in low gear with one of the easiest and most delicious of all Italian antipasti. The ham must be cut paper thin and the melon sweet.

INGREDIENTS FOR 6 CYCLISTS

- 1 large ripe cantaloupe or honeydew melon
  12 slices Parma ham or San Danielle ham
- black pepper

PLAYBOOK

1. Cut melon in half.
2. Remove all seeds.
▲ 3. Cut each half into six slivers and remove the skin from each slice with a sharp knife.
4. Arrange melon slices on individual plates or a serving platter.
◆ 5. Lay a ham slice on each melon piece and sprinkle with pepper.

Serve.

COACH'S CORNER
- *Can also use fresh figs, if available.*
- *Use a pepper grinder, if possible.*
▲ *Use a paring knife or a grapefruit knife.*
◆ *For easy handling, take the ham out of the refrigerator 2–3 hours before using.*

INGREDIENTS
FOR 6–8 GOLFERS

1 pound smoked salmon

6–8 slices white or whole wheat
bread, toasted

SAUCE

• 6 tablespoons mustard

2 lemons, each cut into 4 pieces

■ 3 tablespoons honey

3 tablespoons warm water

4 sprigs of fresh dill (optional)

SMOKED SALMON WITH HONEY MUSTARD SAUCE

A perfect starter to any round, a birdie on
the first hole. Inexpensive, elegant, and simple,
this opening round will win applause from
the crowd.

PLAYBOOK

1. In a small bowl, stir together the mustard,
   honey, and warm water.
2. Spread salmon on individual plates.
3. Drizzle with honey mustard sauce.
4. Garnish each plate with a small piece of dill
   and a lemon wedge.

Serve with toast.

COACH'S CORNER

• *Use good French mustard, such as
Dijon, if available.*

■ *Put honey in microwave for 30 seconds to make it easier to blend.*

CARPACCIO

A simple yet elegant dish, perfect for pro bowlers and fans alike. A specialty of many great restaurants in Tuscany. The secret to this dish is in the quality of the ingredients.

PLAYBOOK

■ 1. Shave very thin slices from the Parmesan cheese.
2. Place the meat slices on a serving platter or individual plates and sprinkle with lemon juice, salt, pepper, and oil.
3. Lay cheese slices on meat.

Serve immediately.

COACH'S CORNER
● *Have butcher cut on a meat slicer and trim fat.*
■ *Put cheese in freezer for 30 minutes. Then slice thin sheets with sharp paring knife, steak knife, vegetable peeler, cheese shaver, or cheese knife.*

---

degree of difficulty: 1
prep time: 5 minutes

INGREDIENTS
FOR 6 TACKLES

2-ounce block Parmesan cheese
● 8 ounces very rare roast beef, sliced paper thin
2 tablespoons fresh lemon juice (optional)
salt and freshly ground pepper
$\frac{1}{4}$ cup extra virgin olive oil

degree of difficulty: 2
prep time: 15 minutes
cooking time: 7–8 minutes

INGREDIENTS FOR 6–8 LINEBACKERS

1½ pounds large shrimp,
    uncooked, shells on
2 cups vinegar
6 cups water
3 tablespoons Old Bay Spice
    Powder (optional)
2 bay leaves (optional)

COCKTAIL SAUCE

1 cup ketchup
3–4 tablespoons horseradish
1 tablespoon lemon juice (optional)

SHRIMP COCKTAIL

An All-American recipe for every occasion.
Make the sauce as mild or hot as you like.

PLAYBOOK

1. In a large pot, bring water and vinegar to a boil.
2. Add optional items.
3. Add shrimp.
4. When water boils again, remove from heat and leave shrimp in the water.
● 5. When shrimp have cooled to a point where you can handle them (10–15 minutes), remove them from the water.
6. Remove shells from shrimp.
■ 7. Make small incision down back of each shrimp and remove vein.

Serve at room temperature, with sauce.

COACH'S CORNER
● *Let them cool off naturally. Do not refrigerate at this point.*
■ *Vein is found just under surface.*

SPARERIBS

Hearty fare for a martial arts champion. Great in the winter by the fire or grilled over the open pit in the summer. Always a favorite with kids of all ages.

PLAYBOOK

1. Combine all ingredients *except* meat in glass or plastic dish.
2. Add spareribs.
3. In refrigerator, marinate 8–10 hours, turning several times.
4. Preheat oven to 350°.
5. Line shallow pan with aluminum foil. Then add spareribs and roast for 45 minutes.
♦ 6. Reduce heat to 325°. Roast 15 minutes more.

Serve.

degree of difficulty: 3
prep time: 15 minutes
cooking time: 60 minutes

INGREDIENTS FOR 4–6 KUNG FU MASTERS

- 2 pounds spareribs, cut into 3 pieces lengthwise
  4 tablespoons soy sauce
- 1 garlic clove, chopped fine
  1 tablespoon sugar
  1 tablespoon ketchup
- ▲ 3 tablespoons hoisin sauce
  2 tablespoons honey

COACH'S CORNER

● *Butcher at supermarket will cut ribs for you.*

■ *Chop with knife or put through garlic press.*

▲ *Available at supermarket, Chinese grocery, or restaurant.*

♦ *Ribs are done when the meat pulls away from the bone.*

degree of difficulty: 3
prep time: 10 minutes
cooking time: 4–7 minutes

INGREDIENTS
FOR 6–8 VAULTERS

1 small loaf French bread

10–12 sun-dried tomatoes packed
   in olive oil

4-inch log of mild, creamy chèvre
   goat cheese

8–10 fresh basil leaves, sliced in half

COACH'S CORNER

● *Toast can be slightly thinner.*

■ *Be careful not to burn rounds. Use a toaster oven, if possible.*

▲ *Use a sharp knife or scissors to cut the tomatoes.*

CHEESE TOASTS WITH BASIL AND SUN-DRIED TOMATOES

You'll clear new heights with this delicious appetizer. A perfect bite-sized snack with drinks or as a topping to a small green salad. Whatever the call, you can't go wrong.

PLAYBOOK

1. *Preheat oven to 375°.*

● 2. Cut the bread into ½-inch rounds.

■ 3. Place the rounds on a large, ungreased baking sheet and toast lightly in the oven for 3–5 minutes or until light brown. Remove from the oven.

4. Raise the oven temperature to broil.

▲ 5. Wipe off excess oil, then finely chop the tomatoes.

6. Spread the cheese on the toasted rounds

7. Sprinkle the top of each round with the chopped tomatoes.

8. Return the baking sheet to the oven and broil the toasts for 1–2 minutes.

9. Place a small piece of basil on each round.

Serve immediately.

BRUSCHETTA: GARLIC TOASTS WITH TOMATOES AND BASIL

degree of difficulty: 2
prep time: 5 minutes
cooking time: 2 minutes

Get the game started with the perfect Italian appetizer. Brings together the simple, rustic tastes of the Tuscan countryside. A great start to a hearty meal.

PLAYBOOK

■ 1. Remove seeds from tomatoes. Chop fine and drain juices.
2. Mix tomatoes, basil, olive oil, and minced garlic.
3. Salt and pepper to taste.
4. Toast bread slices until golden brown.
5. Brush one side of toast lightly with the additional oil, rub with the garlic halves, and top with the tomato mixture.

Serve.

INGREDIENTS FOR 6–8 PLAYERS

4 ripe tomatoes
● ½ cup basil leaves, chopped fine, *or* 1 teaspoon dried basil
3 tablespoons olive oil plus additional for brushing the bread
1 garlic clove, minced
salt and pepper
1 garlic clove, cut in half
1 loaf of crusty, country-style Italian or French bread, sliced ½ inch thick

COACH'S CORNER

● *When using dried herbs, always place them in the palm of your hand, and rub your palms together vigorously. This releases the flavor.*

■ *Use a strainer or your hands to remove as much juice as possible.*

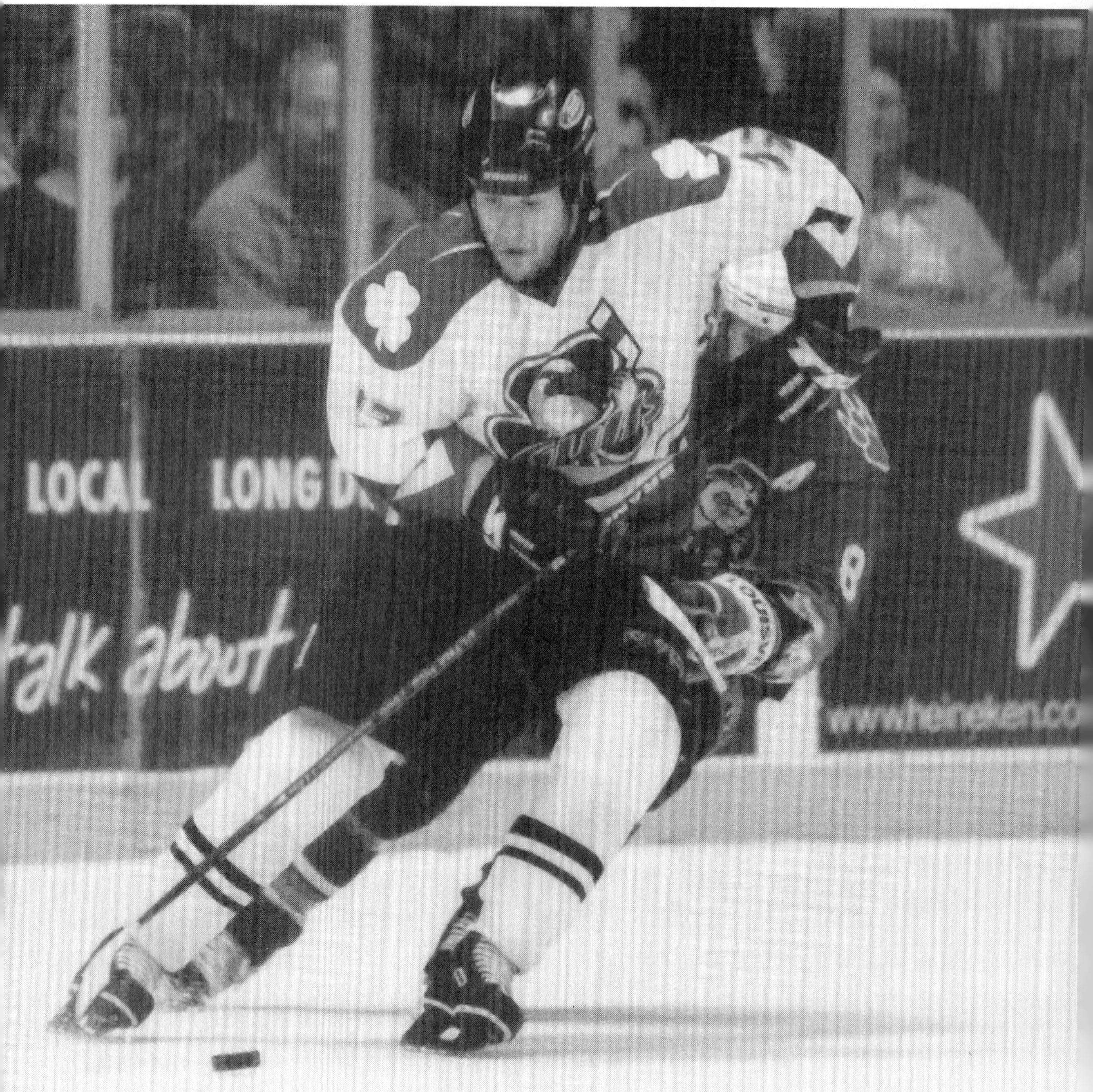
LOCAL
LONG D
talk about
8
www.heineken.co

SOUPS

GAZPACHO

degree of difficulty: 2

prep time: 15 minutes

cooking time: 5 minutes

This refreshing soup is served cold and is as easy as coasting downhill—a perfect summer treat. It keeps well in the refrigerator for at least 3 days, so make an extra portion.

PLAYBOOK

1. Put tomatoes in boiling water for 4 minutes, then plunge them in cold water and remove skins.
2. Blend all ingredients in a blender until smooth.
3. Adjust for seasoning.
4. Chill several hours.

Serve.

INGREDIENTS FOR 6–8 CYCLISTS

- ● 6–7 large ripe tomatoes
- ■ 2 garlic cloves, chopped
  ½ onion, chopped
  1 carrot, coarsely chopped
  salt and pepper
  4 cups tomato juice
- ▲ 1 green pepper, seeded and coarsely chopped
  2 parsley sprigs
  3 tablespoons chopped fresh basil (optional)
  juice of 2 lemons

COACH'S CORNER
- ● *About 1½ pounds.*
- ■ *Cut garlic in half and remove any green center.*
- ▲ *Cut pepper in half and remove seeds.*

---

degree of difficulty: 3
prep time: 10 minutes
cooking time: 50 minutes

INGREDIENTS
FOR 6 FORWARDS

4 medium onions, skins removed

3 tablespoons vegetable oil

½ cup red wine

8 cups chicken broth or beef
   consommé

● 1 cup grated Swiss cheese

2 bay leaves

12 slices French bread, ¼ inch thick

pepper to taste

COACH'S CORNER

● *If possible, use imported
Swiss Emmental or Gru-
yère cheese, available in
most markets.*

■ *Special equipment:
6 ovenproof soup bowls.*

ONION SOUP

A slap shot into the nets with this heartwarming recipe. Often a standard in French restaurants, this game winner is easy in your own arena.

PLAYBOOK

1. Slice the onions thinly.
2. On medium-high setting, heat the oil in a large soup pot and cook the onions, stirring often, until golden brown.
3. Pour the wine into the pot and scrape the bottom of the pot clean. *Do not discard anything from the pot.*
4. Add the broth or consommé, pepper, and bay leaf and continue cooking for 2 minutes.
5. *Reduce heat to low* and continue cooking for 30–40 minutes.
6. Dry the slices of French bread in a 250° oven.
■ 7. Discard the bay leaves and pour the soup into 6 ovenproof bowls.
8. Top each bowl with 2 slices of bread and sprinkle with cheese.
9. Put bowls under broiler and heat until cheese browns.

Serve immediately.

ONION AND TOMATO SOUP

The sweet taste of a slam dunk with this perfect blend of French Provençal and American home-grown flavors. The home team will be begging for more.

PLAYBOOK

- 1. Peel potatoes.
  2. Put tomatoes in boiling water for 4 minutes, then plunge them in cold water and remove skins.
  3. Cut garlic in half and remove any green center.
- 4. Put potatoes, garlic, and tomatoes into a soup pot and cover with water.
  5. Add the salt and pepper and bring to a boil over high heat.
  6. Reduce heat to a simmer.
  7. Cook, covered, for 2 hours.
  8. Cook the onions in the olive oil over low heat. Do not allow them to brown.
  9. In a food mill or blender, purée onions, potatoes, and tomatoes.
  10. Adjust for seasoning.

▲ TO SERVE: Put a slice of toast into each soup bowl and pour in the soup.

degree of difficulty: 4
prep time: 10 minutes
cooking time: 2 hours
15 minutes

INGREDIENTS FOR 6 CENTERS

1½ pounds potatoes, peeled
1½ pounds tomatoes
1 tablespoon salt
1 teaspoon pepper
4 medium onions, chopped
4 tablespoons olive oil
6 pieces of toast
2 garlic cloves, cut in half

COACH'S CORNER

- *Use knife or vegetable peeler.*
- *Add enough cold water to cover tomatoes and potatoes.*
- ▲ *For additional flavor, rub toast with garlic.*

INGREDIENTS
FOR 6 HIGH DIVERS

6 cups chicken broth
1 tablespoon soy sauce
● 1 teaspoon ginger, chopped fine
2 tablespoons cornstarch, dissolved
   in ½ cup water
2 eggs, beaten slightly
1 scallion, chopped fine
salt and pepper to taste
1 cup of cooked asparagus, cut into
   1-inch pieces
1 cup crabmeat
½ teaspoon sesame oil

CRABMEAT AND
ASPARAGUS SOUP

Score a "10" from the judges with this great
blend of hot soup, fresh crabmeat, and asparagus. Can be served with a bowl of steamed rice
to make a larger meal.

PLAYBOOK

■ 1. Bring broth to boil. Add ginger.
▲ 2. Add asparagus, crabmeat, soy sauce, and
    sesame oil.
3. Simmer for 2 minutes. Do not boil!
4. Using fork, blend 2 tablespoons cornstarch
    with water (should be a thin paste with no
    lumps). Add mixture slowly with whisk or
    fork, stirring in dissolved cornstarch. Cook
    30 seconds: soup will thicken.
5. Add eggs, stirring constantly in circular motion.
6. Sprinkle chopped scallion and pepper on top.

Serve immediately.

COACH'S CORNER
● *About 1 inch of ginger with skin
removed.*
■ *Cover pot. Soup boils faster with less
evaporation.*
▲ *Fresh-cooked asparagus preferred over
canned. To cook quickly, place 3–4 stalks
on a plate, cover with plastic wrap, and
microwave at high for 30 seconds.
Canned asparagus does not need to be
cooked.*

PASTA AND BEAN SOUP

You're in the winner's circle when serving the most popular of all Italian soups. A healthy, hearty dish, this soup is great for an after-school snack or for company.

PLAYBOOK

1. Heat oil in a large soup pot over medium heat.
2. Sauté the vegetables for 7 minutes, stirring occasionally, until lightly browned.
3. Add thyme, tomato paste, and salt and pepper.
4. Add water and simmer for 20 minutes.
5. Remove vegetables.
6. In a blender or food processor, purée vegetables and one-half of the beans.
♦ 7. Add purée, remainder of beans, and pasta to the water and cook 10–13 minutes.

Serve.

COACH'S CORNER
- *Cut into small pieces.*
- *Wash under cold running water for 30 seconds. This removes excess salt.*
- ▲ *Judge amount of pasta by total boxed weight.*
- ♦ *Cooking instructions usually appear on the pasta package.*

---

degree of difficulty: **3**
prep time: **15** minutes
cooking time: **40** minutes

INGREDIENTS FOR 6 JOCKEYS

- 1 carrot, washed and diced
- 1 celery stalk, diced
- 2 onions, peeled and diced
- 3 medium-sized potatoes, diced
  1 tablespoon fresh thyme *or*
    1 teaspoon dried thyme
  2 tablespoons tomato paste
  2 tablespoons olive oil
- ■ 2 cans white beans, rinsed
- ▲ 3½ ounces pasta (shells or tortiglioni)
  salt and pepper
  2 quarts water

degree of difficulty: 3
prep time: 15 minutes
cooking time: 15 minutes

INGREDIENTS
FOR 6–8 SURFERS

3 cups corn kernels

3 cups chicken broth

¼ cup chopped fresh cilantro

1 tablespoon extra virgin olive oil

½ cup onion, chopped

● ½ cup red bell pepper, diced

● ½ cup green bell pepper, diced

salt and pepper to taste

1 tablespoon chopped fresh thyme
   leaves

■ ½ pound medium shrimp, peeled
   and deveined

CORN AND
SHRIMP CHOWDER

Ride the crest of the wave with each spoonful. Both elegant and "down-home," this delicious soup is satisfying no matter what the weather.

PLAYBOOK

▲ 1. In a blender, combine 1 cup of corn, 1 cup of broth, and the cilantro. Blend until very smooth.

2. Heat the olive oil in a soup pot over medium heat, then add the onions, peppers, salt, pepper, and thyme.

3. Cook for 3 minutes.

4. Add the blended corn mixture and the remaining 2 cups of broth and 2 cups of corn.

5. Bring to a low boil (or simmer), then add the shrimp.

6. Cover and cook for 5 minutes.

Serve immediately.

> ### COACH'S CORNER
> ● *Cut into small pieces.*
> ■ *See recipe for shrimp cocktail (page 8).*
> ▲ *Important process for achieving proper texture of soup.*

VEGETABLE SALADS

Mozzarella, Tomatoes, and Basil

Tomato and Basil Salad with
Goat Cheese

Blue Cheese Salad

Caesar Salad with Grilled Chicken

Green Beans and Mushrooms
with Walnut Dressing

Green Salad with Parmesan
Cheese Chips

MOZZARELLA, TOMATOES, AND BASIL

As refreshing as a plunge in the Mediterranean, this salad is found in every restaurant along the water's edge. Italian by concept, French by adoption, this salad is now found everywhere.

PLAYBOOK

1. Slice the tomatoes and arrange them on a large serving dish.
2. Cut thin slices of cheese and place on top of each tomato.
3. Place a basil leaf on top of cheese.
4. Sprinkle with olive oil, salt, and pepper.

Serve.

COACH'S CORNER
- *Tomatoes must be firm and ripe.*
- *If possible, use fresh ground pepper.*

---

degree of difficulty: 1
prep time: 5 minutes

INGREDIENTS
FOR 8 SWIMMERS

- 4 large ripe tomatoes
  1 pound fresh mozzarella cheese
  ½ cup extra virgin olive oil
- salt and pepper to taste
  fresh basil leaves

INGREDIENTS FOR 6–8 LEAD-OFF BATTERS

- 6–8 large ripe tomatoes
- small log of goat cheese
  ½ cup extra virgin olive oil
  1 cup loosely packed basil leaves
  salt and freshly ground pepper
    to taste

TOMATO AND BASIL SALAD WITH GOAT CHEESE

Summertime is back in full swing with this delicious and beautiful salad. Pure Italian, with its colors of red, green, and white.

PLAYBOOK

1. Slice the tomatoes and arrange them on individual plates.
2. Place a thin slice of cheese on each tomato.
3. Place one or two basil leaves on each tomato.
4. Sprinkle with oil.
5. Season with salt and pepper.

Serve with fresh French bread, preferably sourdough.

COACH'S CORNER

- *Tomatoes must be ripe for the salad to be tasty.*
- *Available in cheese department of supermarket or gourmet shop.*

BLUE CHEESE SALAD

This salad packs the punch of a heavyweight champion, but it's easy to prepare and is perfect for any meal.

PLAYBOOK

DRESSING

Place dressing ingredients in a bowl and blend until smooth. Set aside.

SALAD

1. Trim any rind from the cheese.
2. Place cheese in the freezer for 25–30 minutes for easier cutting.
3. Remove the cheese from the freezer and cut it into $\frac{1}{4}$–$\frac{1}{2}$-inch cubes.
4. Remove and discard the stems from the spinach. Wash the leaves well and then dry them with paper towels or a kitchen towel.
5. Cut the radishes into thin slices.
6. Combine the spinach, radish slices, and walnut pieces in a serving bowl.
7. Pour the dressing over the salad and toss.

Serve.

degree of difficulty: 3
prep time: 30 minutes

INGREDIENTS
FOR 6 CHAMPIONS

6 ounces of any blue cheese
- 1$\frac{1}{2}$ pounds fresh spinach
- $\frac{3}{4}$ cup walnut pieces (crushed)
1 cup red radishes (optional)

DRESSING

$\frac{1}{4}$ cup walnut oil
$\frac{1}{4}$ cup olive oil
2 tablespoons lemon juice
1 teaspoon mustard
salt and pepper to taste

COACH'S CORNER

- *Spinach for this salad is uncooked. It should be washed two or three times and then dried with a towel.*
- *Use crushed walnuts or place whole walnut pieces between two sheets of waxed paper or kitchen towel and crush with the bottom of a frying pan.*

degree of difficulty: 3

prep time: 15 minutes

cooking time: 15 minutes

INGREDIENTS FOR
6 POWER FORWARDS

1 head of Romaine lettuce

1 tablespoon mustard

3 tablespoons olive oil

1 garlic clove, peeled

2 tablespoons red wine vinegar

4 tablespoons vegetable oil

1 cup grated Parmesan cheese

6 slices French bread

4 tablespoons melted, unsalted
   butter

1 teaspoon salt

2 grilled chicken breasts (optional)

● black pepper

COACH'S CORNER

● *Freshly ground or crushed black pepper is preferable.*

CAESAR SALAD
WITH GRILLED CHICKEN

This salad combines the power and muscle of a basketball team. It is chock-full of strong flavors and serves as a great beginning to a hearty meal.

PLAYBOOK

CROUTONS

1. Cut the slices of bread into 1–1½-inch cubes.
2. Heat the vegetable oil and butter together in a pan until they sizzle.
3. Put bread cubes in a pan and fry for 2 minutes or until golden brown.
4. Drain on paper towel and sprinkle with 2 tablespoons of grated Parmesan cheese. Set aside.

CHICKEN

1. Flatten the breasts with the bottom of a frying pan.
2. Grill under broiler for 3–4 minutes on each side.
3. Cut into thin strips and set aside.

SALAD

1. Rub the inside of a large salad bowl with the garlic.
2. Add the mustard, vinegar, olive oil, salt, pepper, and 2 tablespoons of the Parmesan cheese. Mix well.
3. Wash and dry the lettuce.
4. Cut the lettuce into 2-inch pieces and add it to the salad bowl.
5. Place chicken strips on top of salad. Sprinkle on the remaining Parmesan cheese; add the croutons and mix well.

Serve on cold plates.

GREEN BEANS AND MUSHROOMS WITH WALNUT DRESSING

degree of difficulty: 2
prep time: 10 minutes
cooking time: 2 minutes

You'll wear the green jacket when you roll in this par on the 18th green. A beautiful salad with golf course colors. Green beans and white mushrooms make for the best taste and appearance.

PLAYBOOK

1. Remove the ends of beans and cut them in half.
● 2. Cook beans in boiling water for 2 minutes. Add cold water to the pot to stop cooking.
3. Wipe off mushrooms with damp paper towel, slice into strips, and sprinkle with lemon juice.
■ 4. In a blender or food processor, purée the walnuts, mustard, vinegar, salt, and pepper.
5. Add the oil and blend well.
6. In a bowl, combine green beans and mushrooms.
7. Add the dressing.

Serve.

INGREDIENTS FOR 6 PLAYERS

1 pound thin, fresh string beans
1 pound large white mushrooms
juice of 2 lemons
¼ cup vegetable oil
1 tablespoon mustard, preferably Dijon
2 tablespoons red wine vinegar
2 tablespoons walnut pieces
salt and pepper to taste

COACH'S CORNER

● *Remove one with a fork. If not cooked, return it to the water for another 30 seconds.*
■ *If food processor is not available, put the nuts in a paper bag or kitchen towel and crush them with a mallet or the bottom of a frying pan.*

degree of difficulty: 2

prep time: 5 minutes

cooking time: 10 minutes

INGREDIENTS FOR
6 DOWNHILL RACERS

6 teaspoons grated Parmesan
   cheese

6–8 ounces mixed greens, sold in
   grocery stores as mesclun or
   spring mix

¼ cup extra virgin olive oil

1 tablespoon mustard, preferably
   Dijon

2 tablespoons vinegar (red wine
   or raspberry)

salt and pepper to taste

● 1 tablespoon pine nuts (optional)

COACH'S CORNER

● *These give the salad an
extra crunch.*

■ *Cheese will melt down
flat and will become crispy
after it dries, in about 1
minute.*

GREEN SALAD
WITH PARMESAN
CHEESE CHIPS

Feel the wind in your face with the freshness of
this crisp and crunchy salad. These easy chips
were once a secret of the best restaurants.
Now they can be made in minutes in your
own kitchen.

PLAYBOOK

PARMESAN CHIPS

1. *Preheat oven to 350°.*
2. Grease a cookie sheet with 1 tablespoon olive
   oil.
■ 3. Place rounded teaspoons of freshly grated
   cheese on buttered sheet and cook in oven 10
   minutes or until brown.
4. Remove chips with a spatula and put on a
   plate to cool.

SALAD

1. Blend together olive oil, mustard, and
   vinegar.
2. In a large bowl, toss greens and salad
   dressing.
3. Add salt and pepper to taste.
4. Divide onto 6 plates and place Parmesan
   chip on top of each.

Serve.

SEAFOOD SALADS

Shrimp and Potato Salad

Curried Seafood Salad

Pasta Salad with Shrimp
and Pine Nuts

Shrimp and Crabmeat Salad

Salade Niçoise

SHRIMP AND POTATO SALAD

degree of difficulty: 3
prep time: 15 minutes
cooking time: 25 minutes

You'll roll a strike every time you take to the lanes with this super salad. Easy to make and a real treat for family and friends.

PLAYBOOK

1. Cut potatoes into bite-sized pieces (in either halves or quarters).
2. In a bowl, mix onion, parsley, and garlic.
3. Slowly add olive oil and blend with whisk or fork until ingredients are combined.
4. Cook, shell, and devein shrimp.
5. Cut shrimp in half and marinate in sauce for 1 hour.
6. Add potatoes to shrimp and toss lightly.
7. Mound the salad on one or two lettuce leaves for each serving.
8. Place 1 or 2 olives on top of salad.

Serve.

INGREDIENTS FOR 6–8 BOWLERS

- 8–10 small potatoes, washed and boiled
- 1 onion, chopped fine
- ¼ cup parsley, chopped
- 1 pound raw shrimp, unpeeled
- 2 garlic cloves, chopped fine
- salt and pepper to taste
- ¾ cup extra virgin olive oil
- lettuce leaves
- 12 green olives, pits removed

COACH'S CORNER

- *Place potatoes in boiling water for 10 minutes. Remove 1, cut in half, and test for doneness.*
- *See recipe for shrimp cocktail (page 8).*

INGREDIENTS FOR 6 TENNIS PLAYERS

SALAD

- ● ½ pound medium peeled shrimp, cooked
  ½ pound lump crabmeat
- ■ ½ pound sea scallops, cut in half and poached
  4 scallions, chopped
  1 cup celery, chopped fine
  6 leaves Romaine lettuce

DRESSING

3 tablespoons mayonnaise
- ▲ ¼ cup mango chutney
  1 tablespoon lemon juice
- ◆ 1 tablespoon mild curry powder
  ½ teaspoon salt
- ✦ ½ fresh mango or peach, chopped

CURRIED SEAFOOD SALAD

Score the match point with this international favorite. Brings together wonderful seafood flavors and the mild chutney flavors of Asia. Larger portions with fresh herb bread can make an elegant dinner.

PLAYBOOK

1. Place the cooked shrimp, crabmeat, scallops, scallions, and celery in a large mixing bowl.
2. To make the dressing, combine the ingredients in a separate bowl and mix. Pour the dressing over the seafood and vegetables and toss gently.
3. Line a platter with lettuce leaves and arrange salad on top.

Serve.

COACH'S CORNER

- ● *See recipe for shrimp cocktail (page 8).*
- ■ *Cook in water that is barely boiling, 10–15 minutes. Test one for doneness.*
- ▲ *Available in all supermarkets.*
- ◆ *Available in supermarkets or Indian restaurants.*
- ✦ *Must be fresh and sweet; otherwise, omit from salad.*

PASTA SALAD WITH SHRIMP AND PINE NUTS

degree of difficulty: 3
prep time: 15 minutes
cooking time: 20 minutes

Your pitch is down the middle with this interesting and versatile recipe. Can be made ahead for a packed lunch, simple snack, or candlelight dinner.

PLAYBOOK

- 1. Blend together the dressing ingredients.
- 2. Prepare shrimp.
  3. Place the pine nuts in a dry medium-sized sauté pan over low heat. Toast the nuts until golden, 5–10 minutes, stirring often. Set aside to cool.
  4. Cut the red pepper into strips and then small pieces.
  5. Cut the scallions on the bias into ¼-inch slices.
  6. Add scallions, red peppers, and pine nuts to the shrimp.

FETTUCCINE

1. Bring a large pot of water to a boil.
2. Cook the pasta according to package directions.
3. Drain the pasta and rinse in cool water to stop cooking.
4. Immediately add the dressing and salad.
5. Toss thoroughly.

Serve at room temperature.

INGREDIENTS FOR 6–8 PITCHERS

DRESSING
½ cup olive oil
¼ cup lemon juice
1 tablespoon Dijon-style mustard
½ cup chopped fresh parsley
salt and freshly ground pepper to taste

SALAD
1 pound medium raw shrimp, unpeeled
6 tablespoons pine nuts
2 medium red bell peppers
4 scallions (white part and 3–4 inches of green)
12 ounces fresh fettuccine

COACH'S CORNER
- *Use a blender, a whisk, or a fork.*
- *See recipe for shrimp cocktail (page 8).*

INGREDIENTS FOR 6 VOLLEYBALL PLAYERS

DRESSING

1 cup mayonnaise

2 tablespoons fresh-squeezed
   lemon juice

½ teaspoon salt

½ teaspoon ground black pepper

¾ cup finely chopped dill
   (optional)

SALAD

1¾ pounds raw shrimp

1 pound lump crabmeat

● 1 celery stalk, washed and chopped
   small

½ onion, minced

lettuce (for garnish)

SHRIMP AND CRABMEAT SALAD

A powerful slam shot means a winning game. This is a tasty salad, combining two great wonders of the sea. Elegant as a first course; fabulous as a main course.

PLAYBOOK

1. Mix the dressing ingredients together in a separate bowl.
■ 2. Prepare the shrimp.
3. Place the shrimp, crabmeat, celery, and onion in a large salad bowl.
4. Pour the dressing over the salad and mix gently with your hands until all the seafood is coated.

Serve the salad in the center of a plate.

COACH'S CORNER

● *Remove and discard celery leaves.*
■ *See recipe for shrimp cocktail (page 8).*

SALADE NIÇOISE

degree of difficulty: 4
prep time: 20 minutes
cooking time: 15 minutes

This is a grand slam in any league. Developed in Nice, France, it combines the flavors of the French Riviera and fresh farm produce. It takes some effort to prepare, but it is always a crowd pleaser.

PLAYBOOK

VINAIGRETTE

1. Combine the lemon juice, vinegar, garlic, mustard, herbs, and salt and pepper to taste.
2. Blend in the olive oil with fork or whisk.

SALAD

1. Cut the cooked potatoes in half and toss with the vinaigrette in a large salad bowl.
2. Add the remaining vegetables, eggs, and anchovies.
3. Crumble in the tuna.
4. Mix thoroughly.

Serve on cold plates.

INGREDIENTS
FOR 4–6 SLUGGERS

VINAIGRETTE

2 tablespoons fresh lemon juice
3 tablespoons red wine vinegar
1 garlic clove, minced
1 teaspoon Dijon mustard
salt and pepper
3 tablespoons extra virgin olive oil
2 tablespoons chopped basil, parsley, sage, tarragon, thyme, or any combination

SALAD

● 8–10 small potatoes, washed and boiled
1 small head Boston lettuce, bottom cut off, washed and torn into medium pieces
2 or 3 carrots, washed and sliced thin
■ 4 or 5 firm, ripe tomatoes, cut into quarters
½ pound green beans boiled 2–3 minutes, until crisp/tender
▲ 3 eggs, hard-boiled
1 green or red pepper, seeds removed, then thinly sliced
One 6½-ounce can water-packed white or light tuna, water drained off
2 anchovy filets (canned), rinsed and chopped (optional)

COACH'S CORNER

● *Place potatoes in boiling water for 10 minutes. Remove, cut in half, and taste to determine doneness.*
■ *If tomatoes seem too large, cut in half again.*
▲ *Place eggs (shell on) into boiling water for 11 minutes. Then plunge them into cold water. When cool, remove shells.*

CHICKEN

French Roasted Chicken with Herbs de Provence

Roasted Chicken in White Wine

Grilled Chicken Italiano

Country-Style Chicken

Honey Chicken

Sautéed Chicken in Mustard Sauce

FRENCH ROASTED CHICKEN WITH HERBS DE PROVENCE

degree of difficulty: 2
prep time: 10 minutes
cooking time: 1 hour
10 minutes

Jump in and test the water with one of the best and easiest of all French chicken recipes. Your home will be filled with the mouth-watering aromas of the fresh herbs.

PLAYBOOK

1. Preheat oven to 400°.
2. Rinse and dry the chicken thoroughly with paper towels.
3. In a bowl, mix all other ingredients.
4. With your fingers, rub the mixture over the outside of the chicken.
▲ 5. Put chicken in ovenproof dish and roast, uncovered, until done.

INGREDIENTS FOR 4 WATER SKIERS

- One 3–4-pound fresh chicken
- 1 tablespoon fresh rosemary leaves
- 1 tablespoon fresh thyme
- 2 tablespoons fresh basil
- 1 tablespoon fresh tarragon leaves
  1 teaspoon salt
  1 tablespoon pepper, coarsely ground preferred
  ¼ cup extra virgin olive oil
  2 garlic cloves, minced

COACH'S CORNER

- *Fresh—not frozen.*
- *When using dried herbs, use only ½ the amount of fresh herbs required and rub between your palms before using (releases flavor).*
- Herbs de Provence *sold in jars— excellent substitute for individual herbs.*
- ▲ *Three-pound chicken—1 hour and 10 minutes. Four-pound chicken—1 hour and 20 minutes.*

degree of difficulty: **4**

prep time: **20** minutes

cooking time: **45** minutes

INGREDIENTS
FOR 6 GYMNASTS

- ½ cup imported dried mushrooms
  1 cup water
  One 3-pound roasting chicken, cut up, *or* 5 plump chicken breasts
  1 tablespoon flour
  ½ stick butter
  3 tablespoons vegetable oil
- ■ 1 cup dry white wine
  salt and pepper

COACH'S CORNER

● *If available, use dried porcini mushrooms.*

■ *Always cook with a wine you are willing to drink. Save remainder of wine for dinner.*

▲ *Leave the bottom inch of water in the bowl—it contains the soil from the mushrooms.*

ROASTED CHICKEN IN WHITE WINE

Family and friends will say you're ready for the Olympics when they taste this great recipe. Follow the Playbook and the whole team will win medals.

PLAYBOOK

1. Place the mushrooms in a bowl with 2 cups of water and let soak for about 15 minutes.
2. Wash the chicken pieces and pat them dry with a paper towel.
3. Heat the butter and oil in a pan large enough to hold all the pieces without overlapping.
4. Put flour in plastic bag, add chicken, and shake to coat the pieces lightly.
5. When the butter and oil are hot, add the floured pieces to the pan and brown over high heat on all sides for about 5 minutes, turning them frequently to avoid sticking.
6. When browned, add the wine and reduce the heat to simmer (low).
▲ 7. Add the mushrooms with their water.
8. Cover the pan and cook for about 20 minutes.
9. Add salt and pepper and continue cooking slowly for 20 minutes longer.

Serve, using pan liquids as sauce.

GRILLED CHICKEN ITALIANO

degree of difficulty: 2
prep time: 15 minutes
cooking time: 10–12 minutes

Another game-winning R.B.I. with a dish that hints of the great Italian Riviera town of Porto-fino, where lemon trees and hedges of rose-mary line the road.

PLAYBOOK

1. *Preheat broiler for 15 minutes.*
● 2. Between two pieces of waxed paper, pound flat each chicken breast.
3. Make a marinade with all other ingredients; blend well with fork in order to incorporate the oil. Put the chicken into the marinade for 2 hours, turning over after 1 hour.
4. Take chicken out of marinade and place 4–5 inches under the broiler.
5. Allow to cook for about 5–6 minutes on each side, spooning on the marinade to keep moist.

Serve hot.

INGREDIENTS FOR 4–6 CLEAN-UP BATTERS

4–5 *skinless and boneless* chicken breasts
3 tablespoons olive oil
1 lemon cut into 8 slices
1 garlic clove, crushed with the back of a spoon
1 sprig of fresh rosemary, *or* 1 teaspoon dried rosemary
salt and pepper
1 bay leaf, crushed
zest of 1 lemon (optional)
2 sun-dried tomatoes, chopped (optional)

COACH'S CORNER
● *Use the bottom of a frying pan to flatten chicken. This enables the chicken to cook evenly and retain its moistness.*

degree of difficulty: 4

prep time: 20 minutes

cooking time: 50 minutes

INGREDIENTS FOR
4 RODEO RIDERS

- 2½ pounds of chicken pieces—
  breasts, legs, and thighs

  3 tablespoons extra virgin olive oil

  2 medium carrots, sliced thin
  (⅛ inch)

  2 garlic cloves, sliced thin

  4 tablespoons minced shallots
- ½ pound white potatoes

  2 ripe tomatoes, chopped, with
  seeds removed

  3 cups chicken broth

  1 cup dry white wine

  1 bay leaf
- ▲ salt and pepper to taste

COACH'S CORNER

● *Select the chicken parts
you and your guests like to
eat. This recipe should be
cooked with skin on and
bones intact.*

■ *Cut into 1-inch chunks.*

▲ *Adjust salt carefully.
The chicken broth contains
salt.*

◆ *Discard bay leaf before
serving.*

COUNTRY-STYLE
FRENCH CHICKEN

Ride 'em, cowgirl! The south of France is well
known for its plentiful sunshine, fruity olive
oil, bountiful herbs, tasty vegetables, and
delicious, hearty recipes.

PLAYBOOK

1. *Preheat oven to 350°.*
2. Rinse and pat dry all chicken parts.
3. In a large ovenproof pan, heat olive oil to
   sizzle.
4. Brown chicken on both sides, then remove.
5. *In same pan*, sauté carrots, garlic, and shallots
   on medium heat for 3–4 minutes, until garlic
   browns and shallots become soft.
6. Pour in wine. Raise heat and scrape the bits
   from the bottom and sides of pan.
◆ 7. Add chicken, broth, tomatoes, potatoes, and
   bay leaf.
8. Put cover on pot and cook in preheated oven
   for 40 minutes.
9. Taste and add salt and pepper, if needed.

Serve immediately.

HONEY CHICKEN

degree of difficulty: **3**
prep time: **5** minutes
cooking time: **40** minutes

Clear the bar for a new meet record. This fabulous little recipe makes a great meal. With just a hint of Asia, it is a flexible dish that can be served with any combination of vegetables.

PLAYBOOK

1. Heat oil in a heavy pan. Add scallion and ginger; stir-fry 1 minute.
2. Brown chicken sections quickly, then drain off excess oil.
3. Combine water, sherry, honey, soy sauce, and salt.

●■ 4. Slowly pour mixture over chicken and simmer, covered, until done, about 40 minutes.

Serve.

COACH'S CORNER
● *Reduce heat to low. Cooking liquid should not boil.*
■ *Breasts cook faster than dark meat. Remove breasts when done.*

INGREDIENTS FOR 6 VAULTERS

3 pounds chicken breasts, legs, or thighs, cut up into bite-sized portions
3–4 tablespoons peanut oil
½ cup sherry
1 scallion, cut in ½-inch pieces
2 tablespoons honey
½ cup water
1 teaspoon fresh ginger, peeled and minced
2 tablespoons soy sauce
1 teaspoon salt

degree of difficulty: 2
prep time: 10 minutes
cooking time: 25 minutes

INGREDIENTS FOR
6 DOWNHILL RACERS

4–6 boned, skinless chicken breasts,
    cut into long slices
salt and pepper
3 tablespoons butter
1 cup dry white wine
½ cup light cream
• 2 tablespoons mustard

COACH'S CORNER
• *Use a French Dijon
mustard, if possible.*
■ *Cooking time varies
with thickness of chicken.
Cut at thickest part to
determine doneness.
Cooked meat will be white.*
▲ *If sauce gets too thick,
stir in a little water to
thin it.*

SAUTÉED CHICKEN
IN MUSTARD SAUCE

A perfect finish for a day on the slopes. The
mustard becomes mild and gentle in the cooking process and adds an exhilarating taste to
the chicken.

PLAYBOOK

■ 1. In a large skillet, sauté the chicken pieces
    in butter over moderately high heat for 4–5
    minutes on each side.
  2. Transfer the chicken to a heated platter and
    keep warm.
  3. Add wine to the pan and "deglaze" the pan,
    scraping up the brown bits clinging to the
    bottom and sides.
▲ 4. Add cream and mustard.
  5. Simmer the mixture, stirring, until it is well
    reduced and thickened.
  6. Add salt and pepper to taste.
  7. Spoon the sauce over the chicken.

Serve.

BEEF AND VEAL

Pepper Steak

Beef with Scallions

Veal Marsala

Veal Chops with Garlic
and Rosemary

Ground Steak with Blue Cheese
and Green Peppercorn Sauce

Pan-Seared Veal Chops with
Brandy Mustard Sauce

PEPPER STEAK

A slap shot from the point scores a goal every time with this hearty dish. You control the game by the amount of heat. Some like a crust of pepper, while others prefer just a hint.

PLAYBOOK

1. Press the crushed pepper into both sides of the steaks.
2. Select a heavy frying pan large enough to hold all of the steaks at one time.
3. Heat ½ the butter on moderate-high heat until it sizzles.
4. Sear (fry) the steaks over high heat for 1½ minutes on each side.
5. Reduce the heat to moderate and cook the steaks for 1 minute more on each side.
6. Remove steaks and sprinkle them with salt.
7. In the same pan, heat the brandy, ignite it with a match, and shake the pan until the flames go out.
■ 8. Add beef broth and the remaining butter and reduce the sauce over high heat to ½ cup.
9. Pour sauce over the steaks.

Serve.

degree of difficulty: 4
prep time: 10 minutes
cooking time: 10 minutes

INGREDIENTS FOR 4–6 DEFENSEMEN

4 New York strip steaks, each 1 inch thick
● 1½ tablespoons crushed black pepper
1 stick butter, cut into small pieces
¼ cup brandy
2 cups canned beef broth
salt

COACH'S CORNER

● *Buy crushed pepper, or place whole pepper-corns between two sheets of waxed paper and crush them with a mallet or the bottom of a pan.*

■ *As the sauce cooks, scrape up the little pieces from the bottom of the pan. They add flavor to the sauce.*

INGREDIENTS
FOR 6 GOLFERS

1 pound flank steak, cut into slices
    $\frac{1}{8}$ inch thick

● 1 tablespoon cornstarch or
    arrowroot

$\frac{1}{2}$ cup water

■ 12 scallions, cut into 1$\frac{1}{2}$-inch pieces

$\frac{1}{4}$ cup chicken broth

2 tablespoons soy sauce

4–6 tablespoons vegetable oil

$\frac{1}{2}$ teaspoon sesame oil

2 cups broccoli (optional)

BEEF WITH SCALLIONS

Your short game puts you right on the green.
A great recipe with a mild hint of Asian
flavoring that has you in the clubhouse with
the low score.

PLAYBOOK

1. In a frying pan, heat $\frac{1}{2}$ of the oil until it
   smokes.
2. Stir in beef for about 30 seconds (until it
   begins to change color). Remove and place
   on paper towels.
3. Add remaining oil. When oil begins to
   smoke, put in scallions. Add broccoli if
   desired. Stir-fry vigorously for about 1
   minute.
4. Add soy sauce and chicken broth and stir for
   30 seconds.
■ 5. Mix cornstarch or arrowroot with the water
   and stir in sauce 1–2 minutes.
▲ 6. Return beef to pan. Stir for about $\frac{1}{2}$ minute.

Serve at once.

COACH'S CORNER
● *Arrowroot is found in small jars in the*
spice section of the supermarket.
■ *Remove small root end of scallions.*
▲ *Do not overcook the beef.*

VEAL MARSALA

degree of difficulty: 4
prep time: 15 minutes
cooking time: 15 minutes

Short to second to first, an easy double play. Thin slivers of veal are blended with the rich taste of Italian wine to produce one of the country's most famous recipes.

PLAYBOOK

- 1. Between 2 layers of waxed paper, place veal, one slice at a time, and beat with a mallet or the bottom of a frying pan until about ⅛ inch thick.
- 2. On a flat surface, spread flour.
  3. Coat both sides of each piece and shake to remove any excess flour.
  4. In a large frying pan, melt ½ of the butter and oil.
- ▲ 5. When butter and oil are very hot, cook 2 or 3 pieces of veal at a time, 30–60 seconds on each side. Move the meat with a spatula to prevent from sticking.
  6. Transfer the slices to a warm plate and cook the rest of the meat.
  7. *In the same pan,* stir together the juice from the plate, the wine, and the other ½ of the butter, scraping up all particles on the bottom of the pan.
  8. Add salt and pepper to the sauce and then pour it over the meat.

Serve.

INGREDIENTS FOR 6 INFIELDERS

2 pounds veal scaloppine
5 tablespoons butter
3 tablespoons vegetable oil
4 tablespoons flour
½ cup Marsala wine
salt and black pepper

COACH'S CORNER

- *Alternatively, have the butcher flatten the meat for you.*
- *Put waxed paper down first to simplify cleanup.*
▲ *The pieces of meat should not overlap.*

degree of difficulty: 2
prep time: 10 minutes
cooking time: 15 minutes

INGREDIENTS FOR
4 TENNIS PLAYERS

4 veal chops, ½ inch thick
3 tablespoons olive oil
4 garlic cloves, minced
● 2 teaspoons rosemary, chopped
　　fine, or 1 teaspoon dried
　　rosemary
2 tablespoons butter
salt
■ lemon, cut into 4 wedges (optional)

VEAL CHOPS WITH GARLIC AND ROSEMARY

The championship is yours with a drop shot at the net. One of the best and easiest of all Italian recipes blends the classic flavors of garlic and rosemary.

PLAYBOOK

1. *Preheat broiler.*
2. In a bowl, mix the olive oil, rosemary, and garlic with a fork.
3. Take one chop at a time and rub each with the oil mixture.
4. Place chops on a broiler pan 5–6 inches from heat.
5. When the chops have formed a nice golden crust, after about 6–7 minutes, turn them.
6. When browned on both sides, remove to plate.
7. Sprinkle with salt and pepper.

Serve lemon wedges on the side.

COACH'S CORNER
● *Dried herbs must be rubbed between your palms before using.*
■ *A fresh squeeze of lemon enhances the flavor of the veal.*

GROUND STEAK WITH BLUE CHEESE AND GREEN PEPPERCORN SAUCE

degree of difficulty: **4**
prep time: **10** minutes
cooking time: **20** minutes

A three-on-one power play: The combination of hearty blue cheese, delicate green peppercorns, and sweet balsamic vinegar transforms the common hamburger into an elegant dish.

PLAYBOOK

1. In a bowl, thoroughly mix meat, eggs, shallots, salt, and pepper.
2. Divide mixture into 6 or 12 patties and flatten slightly.
3. Heat a heavy frying pan.
4. Add the oil and cook one side of the meat over medium-high.
◆ 5. Turn each patty and cook until almost done.
6. Cover each patty with cheese.
7. Continue cooking until the cheese melts.
8. Put meat on a warm plate.
9. Pour off fat from frying pan.
▲ 10. Add the vinegar and scrape off bottom of pan. *Do not discard liquids.*
11. Add peppercorns and cream. Whisk in the butter, one small piece at a time. Cook over medium heat until sauce begins to thicken.

Spoon sauce over each patty and serve.

INGREDIENTS FOR 6 POINT MEN

- • 3 pounds coarsely chopped beef
  2 eggs, lightly beaten with fork
  2 shallots, chopped
  1½ teaspoons salt
  1½ teaspoons pepper
- ■ ½ cup blue cheese, crumbled
  3 tablespoons vegetable oil
- ▲ ½ cup balsamic vinegar
  3–4 tablespoons green peppercorns
  1 cup heavy cream
  ½ stick butter, cut into small pieces

COACH'S CORNER

- • *Buy the best quality, lowest fat meat.*
- ■ *Roquefort is the favored blue cheese for this recipe.*
- ▲ *Port wine can be substituted for the vinegar.*
- ◆ *Check to see whether meat is cooked to your taste before proceeding further.*

degree of difficulty: 3
prep time: 10 minutes
cooking time: 30 minutes

INGREDIENTS FOR
4–6 POLE VAULTERS

2 tablespoons extra virgin olive oil

4–6 lean veal chops, 8–10 ounces each

pepper to taste

2 shallots, minced

● 1 cup chopped wild mushrooms (cremini, portabello, or shiitake)

¾ cup canned chicken broth

¼ cup brandy

1 tablespoon tomato paste

■ 1 tablespoon chopped fresh tarragon

1 tablespoon mustard

COACH'S CORNER

● *Any mushroom or combination of mushrooms will work very well.*

■ *If using dried tarragon, use ½ teaspoon and rub between palms before putting tarragon into sauce.*

PAN-SEARED VEAL CHOPS WITH BRANDY MUSTARD SAUCE

Clear the high bar with this elegant and delicious recipe. The easy technique seals in the flavors and juices. Of Italian origins, this great dish is found wherever great food is available.

PLAYBOOK

1. *Preheat oven to 400°.*
2. Heat the olive oil in a frying pan and, when hot, sear the veal chops on both sides until golden brown.
3. Transfer to an ovenproof dish and bake in the oven for 15 minutes. *Do not discard cooking liquids from the frying pan.*

SAUCE

1. While the meat is in the oven, prepare the sauce in the frying pan by adding the mushrooms, shallots, broth, brandy, tomato paste, and tarragon.
2. Cook over medium heat until the sauce is reduced by one-half.
3. Stir in the mustard and remove from the heat.

Spoon the sauce over veal chops and serve.

FISH

Grilled Salmon with Mustard and Tarragon

Broiled Rockfish with Fennel and Walnut Oil

Grilled Swordfish with Capers, Lemon, and Garlic

Tuna Wrapped in Bacon

Grilled Swordfish with Salsa

Steamed Rockfish or Sea Bass with Black Beans

GRILLED SALMON WITH MUSTARD AND TARRAGON

degree of difficulty: **4**

prep time: **15** minutes

cooking time: **5–10** minutes

Mustard and tarragon, both strong flavors, become gentle giants when fused with the superb delicacy of fresh salmon.

PLAYBOOK

THE NIGHT BEFORE

1. Prepare the marinade by mixing together mustard, olive oil, brown sugar, tarragon, salt, and pepper.
2. Wipe the salmon dry with paper towels.
3. Put fish in a glass dish.
4. With a sharp knife, cut salmon through *halfway* to skin, creating 6 equal pieces.
5. Pour the marinade over the fish.
6. Cover the fish with foil and put it in refrigerator until ready to prepare.

TO COOK

1. Preheat broiler for 15 minutes.
2. Slide salmon onto broiling pan.
◆ 3. Place broiling pan about 4 inches under the heating element and broil the salmon until cooked, about 5–10 minutes.

Serve with lemon slices.

INGREDIENTS FOR 6 LINEMEN

3 pounds salmon fillets, with skin left on

3 tablespoons Dijon mustard

3 tablespoons olive oil

● 2 tablespoons brown sugar

■ 3 tablespoons fresh tarragon, chopped

1 teaspoon salt

▲ 1 tablespoon pepper

3 lemons, sliced

COACH'S CORNER

● *Available in any supermarket.*

■ *You may substitute 1 tablespoon dried tarragon, rubbing the leaves between the palms before using.*

▲ *Coarse or freshly ground pepper preferred.*

◆ *Cooking time depends on thickness of fish. Fish is done when still moist but separates easily with a fork.*

degree of difficulty: **2**

prep time: **3** minutes

cooking time: **15–20** minutes

INGREDIENTS
FOR 6 CLIMBERS

2–3 rockfish or sea bass fillets,
   skin on one side
- ¼ cup walnut oil
- ■ 1 tablespoon fennel seeds, crushed
- ▲ 2 tablespoons fresh tarragon leaves
   salt and pepper to taste

BROILED ROCKFISH WITH FENNEL AND WALNUT OIL

This is much easier than climbing a mountain. Rockfish is a thick, meaty fish caught in American and French waters. This recipe is perfect in any season.

PLAYBOOK

1. *Preheat broiler for 15 minutes.*
2. Rinse and thoroughly dry the fish.
3. Rub the fish with walnut oil.
4. Sprinkle with fennel seeds.
5. Place the fish on a grilling tray and grill 3–4 inches from the heat.
♦ 6. Cook for 15–20 minutes, until done.
7. Sprinkle with tarragon.

Serve.

COACH'S CORNER
- *Available in any gourmet store.*
- ■ *Put the seeds in waxed paper or paper towel and crush with mallet or the bottom of a frying pan.*
- ▲ *Use ½ of amount with dried herbs. Rub herbs in palm of hand to release flavors.*
- ♦ *Cooked fish should break apart easily with fork.*

GRILLED SWORDFISH WITH CAPERS, LEMON, AND GARLIC

degree of difficulty: 2
prep time: 10 minutes
cooking time: 8–10 minutes

Ninth inning, two out, winning run on third. What do you call? Your best pitch. This recipe is really the fast ball down the middle. Overpower them with blistering ease.

PLAYBOOK

1. *Preheat broiler for 15 minutes.*
■ 2. Rub the swordfish steaks on both sides with 1 tablespoon of olive oil, and lightly salt and pepper them.
3. With a fork, mash together the garlic and capers, then add lemon juice and 1 teaspoon of olive oil. Blend well. Season to taste with pepper. *Set aside.*
▲ 4. Grill the fish or broil 3–4 inches from the heating element for 4–5 minutes on each side. Remove from the heat.
5. Spoon the caper / lemon mixture over each steak.

Serve at once.

INGREDIENTS FOR 4–6 RELIEVERS

● 4 fresh swordfish steaks, ¾ inch thick
1 tablespoon plus 1 teaspoon olive oil
salt and pepper
2 garlic cloves, minced
3 tablespoons capers
juice of 2 lemons

COACH'S CORNER
● *Tastes best with fresh fish.*
■ *Spread oil with the back of a spoon.*
▲ *Fish should be slightly pink inside.*

---

degree of difficulty: 4

prep time: 5 minutes

cooking time: 8 minutes

INGREDIENTS
FOR 6–8 SPRINTERS

- Five or six 6-ounce tuna steaks
- 5–6 bacon slices, uncooked
  2 lemons, each cut into 4 pieces
  2 tablespoons parsley, chopped
- ▲ black pepper

COACH'S CORNER

● *Ask the fishmonger for freshest tuna.*

■ *Used smoked bacon if possible.*

▲ *Fresh ground or coarse ground pepper is preferable.*

TUNA WRAPPED IN BACON

Sprint to the finish line and the crowd will be roaring its approval. The fresh sea taste and mountain smokiness make a winning combination.

PLAYBOOK

1. Season the tuna generously with pepper.
2. Wrap a slice of bacon around the thickest part of each piece of tuna, overlapping the ends by about $\frac{1}{2}$ inch.
3. Secure the bacon on the tuna with toothpicks.
4. Put the butter in a frying pan and cook until it sizzles.
5. Add the tuna and cook until the bacon browns—about 4 minutes.
6. Turn tuna and repeat process of other side.
7. Place finished tuna on a warm platter while other pieces are cooking.
8. Remove the toothpicks.

Serve.

GRILLED SWORDFISH WITH SALSA

degree of difficulty: 1
prep time: 10 minutes
cooking time: 8 minutes

A three-point play to win the game! Nothing is better than freshly grilled swordfish with the tang and zest of the Southwest. Select your own "heat," but use only freshest fish.

PLAYBOOK

1. *Preheat broiler for 15 minutes.*
■ 2. Trim swordfish of any dark or black meat.
3. Rub the steaks with oil and season with salt and pepper.
4. Place swordfish 4–5 inches from broiler.
▲ 5. Broil for 4 minutes on each side, or until lightly browned.
6. Remove fish from broiler and mound 2 tablespoons of salsa on each steak.

Serve with rice.

INGREDIENTS FOR 4 SHOOTING GUARDS

● 4 swordfish steaks, ¾ inch thick
2 tablespoons vegetable or olive oil
salt and black pepper
8 ounces of salsa

COACH'S CORNER

● *Ask the fishmonger for freshest pieces.*
■ *Black portion at bottom of fish is bitter.*
▲ *Remove from broiler and test for doneness. Fish should break off easily and be slightly pink inside.*

degree of difficulty: 4
prep time: 10 minutes
cooking time: 30 minutes

INGREDIENTS
FOR 6–8 SKATERS

2 pounds fresh rockfish or sea bass
   fillets

1 tablespoon white wine

½ teaspoon salt

2 tablespoons minced cooked
   bacon or smoked ham

2 tablespoons vegetable oil

● ½ teaspoon sesame oil

■ 2 scallions, including tops, cut into
   2-inch pieces

● 2 tablespoons fermented black
   beans, washed

4–6 slices fresh ginger, about
   ⅛ inch thick

1 tablespoon chopped fresh garlic

2 tablespoons soy sauce

STEAMED ROCKFISH OR SEA BASS WITH BLACK BEANS

Your guests will be doing triple jumps when this Olympic presentation is put on the table.

PLAYBOOK

1. *Preheat the oven to 400°.*
2. Wash the fish under cold running water and dry well.
3. Mix wine and salt together and rub mixture on both sides of fish.
4. Place the fish on an ovenproof dish large enough to hold the fillets without over-lapping.
5. Spread the rest of the ingredients evenly over the fish.
6. Cover dish tightly with aluminum foil.
▲ 7. Cook for 30 minutes or until done.

Serve at once.

COACH'S CORNER

● *Available in supermarkets, Chinese grocery stores, or restaurants.*

■ *Remove stringy root bottom from scallions.*

▲ *Open foil carefully. Cut off tiny corner of fish to check doneness. It should be white and flake easily.*

SHELLFISH

Crispy Shrimp Wrapped in Bacon

Shrimp with Olive Oil and Lemon

Lobster Medallions with
Chive Sauce

Maryland Crab Cakes

Stir-Fried Scallops with Onions

Sautéed Scallops with Garlic
and Parsley

Steamed Mussels in White Wine
and Herbs

CRISPY SHRIMP WRAPPED IN BACON

degree of difficulty: 6
prep time: 10 minutes
cooking time: 12 minutes

Down the middle for a strike! Crispy shrimp and smoky bacon, just right for any season. The mild yet tangy sauce can be spiced up with a little Tabasco if you like it hot.

PLAYBOOK

■ 1. Shell and devein shrimp.
2. Cut each bacon strip in half and wrap one half around each shrimp.
3. Stick toothpick through shrimp to hold the bacon while cooking.
4. Dip the bacon-wrapped shrimp in beaten egg.
5. Sprinkle lightly with pepper.
6. Heat oil. Pan-fry shrimp on both sides until shrimp are slightly pink and bacon is crisp.
7. Remove toothpicks.
▲ 8. Add sauce ingredients, stirring occasionally, until shrimp are done, about 2 minutes more.

Serve hot.

INGREDIENTS
FOR 6 BOWLERS

● 1½ pounds large shrimp, uncooked
12–15 bacon strips, uncooked
2 beaten eggs mixed with
   1 tablespoon water
¼ teaspoon black pepper
1½ tablespoons vegetable oil
10 toothpicks, cut in half

SAUCE
½ cup ketchup
3 tablespoons Worcestershire Sauce
1 tablespoon red wine vinegar
2 teaspoons sugar
2 tablespoons soy sauce

COACH'S CORNER
● *Use large shrimp, approximately 15–20 to the pound.*
■ *Make small cut down back of shrimp and remove black vein, if any.*
▲ *Shrimp turn pink when done.*

INGREDIENTS FOR 4–6 CLEANUP HITTERS

40 medium-sized raw shrimp

1 cup water

1 cup white wine or white vinegar

⅓ cup extra virgin olive oil

2 tablespoons chopped parsley (optional)

juice of 3 lemons

black pepper

1 garlic clove, minced (optional)

SHRIMP WITH OLIVE OIL AND LEMON

An inside-the-park home run. A dish with the style and grace of a major league player. Simple preparation and brilliant taste.

PLAYBOOK

1. In a large pot, bring water and vinegar or wine to a boil.
2. Add shrimp (*with shells on*).
3. When water boils *again, remove pot from heat*, and leave shrimp in the water.
● 4. When shrimp have cooled to a point where you can handle them (10–15 minutes), remove shrimp from water.
5. Remove shells from shrimp.
■ 6. Cut a small incision down the back of each shrimp and remove vein.
7. Pour the oil and lemon juice over the shrimp.
8. Add parsley and garlic, if desired.
9. Add pepper.

Toss and serve.

COACH'S CORNER
● *Let them cool off naturally. Do not refrigerate at this point.*
■ *Vein is found just under surface.*

LOBSTER MEDALLIONS WITH CHIVE SAUCE

degree of difficulty: 5
prep time: 10 minutes
cooking time: 10 minutes

You're first at the finish line with lobster, one of the most elegant of all dishes. Can also be served as an appetizer or chopped for the topping of a large lunch salad.

PLAYBOOK

1. Slice lobster meat into $\frac{1}{2}$-inch slices.
▲ 2. In a frying pan set on medium-high heat, cook the lobster slices in $\frac{1}{2}$ of the butter for 2 minutes on each side.
3. Remove and cover lobster with plastic wrap to keep warm.

SAUCE

1. Over moderate heat, cook the shallots until soft in the same pan in which the lobster was cooked.
2. Stir in the wine, water, clam juice, and cream.
3. Boil until it thickens enough to form white film on the back of a spoon, 3–4 minutes.
4. Stir $\frac{1}{2}$ of the butter into the sauce one piece at a time.
5. Add the chives, salt, and pepper.
6. Place 2–3 slices of lobster on each plate.
7. With a spoon, ladle sauce over lobster.

Serve.

INGREDIENTS FOR 4–6 HURDLERS

- $2\frac{1}{2}$ pounds lobster tail meat (if frozen, defrost under cold running water)
  1 stick sweet butter (4 ounces)

  SAUCE
  1 shallot, finely chopped
  1 cup dry white wine
- ■ $\frac{1}{2}$ cup clam juice
  $\frac{1}{2}$ cup water
  1 cup light cream
  1 teaspoon chives, chopped
  Salt and pepper

COACH'S CORNER
- *Fresh meat often available in super-market.*
- ■ *Use bottled clam juice.*
- ▲ *Place butter for sauce in the freezer for 10 minutes, then cut into 10 or 12 small pieces.*

degree of difficulty: **4**

prep time: **15** minutes

cooking time: **25** minutes

INGREDIENTS FOR 6–8 GOLFING BUDDIES

1 pound backfin crabmeat

● 1 pound jumbo lump crabmeat

2 tablespoons butter

1 medium sweet red pepper, chopped

1 tablespoon mustard

½ teaspoon salt

1 teaspoon white pepper

2 eggs, lightly beaten

1 cup mayonnaise

COACH'S CORNER

● *Can use backfin crab-meat. Jumbo lump crab-meat consists of larger pieces, but it is more expensive.*

■ *Flatten crab cakes a bit more if using pan-fry method. They will cook more evenly.*

MARYLAND CRAB CAKES

Pitch and roll into the cup on the 18th green with this sensational recipe. Perfect for weekend entertaining.

PLAYBOOK

1. Cut open red pepper, remove seeds, then chop into small pieces.
2. In a small skillet, on medium-high, melt the butter, and sauté the pepper until tender.
3. Place the crabmeat in a large bowl and combine with the cooked pepper, mustard, salt, pepper, eggs, and ¾ of the mayonnaise.
4. Fold the ingredients together gently, being careful not to break up the lumps.
5. Divide the mixture into 6–8 portions.
■ 6. Mold each portion into a ball and then flatten each slightly.

TWO COOKING CHOICES

OVEN BAKE

1. Top each crab cake with a teaspoon of mayonnaise.
2. Bake crab cakes at 350° for 15 minutes.

PAN-FRY (SAUTÉ)

1. Heat, over medium-high, ½ stick of butter (2 ounces) in a frying pan until it sizzles.
2. Cook 3–4 crab cakes at a time, 3–4 minutes on each side.

STIR-FRIED SCALLOPS WITH ONIONS

degree of difficulty: 3
prep time: 15 minutes
cooking time: 15 minutes

Get ready to catch the crowd, hook, line, and sinker. The hint of sesame oil adds a delicate Asian flavor. Can be made ahead and reheated at the last minute.

PLAYBOOK

1. *Do not wash scallops.* Cut in half, removing hard muscle on the side.
2. Salt and pepper scallops and set aside.
- 3. Thinly slice onion.
4. Heat vegetable oil in frying pan over high heat.
- 5. Add onion, stir-frying until soft and brown, about 3 minutes.
6. Put onions on a plate.
7. In the same pan, add scallops and stir-fry over high heat until brown, then reduce heat to medium-low, cover, and cook until done, about 3–4 minutes.
8. Add onions and sesame oil and stir-fry all ingredients for 30 seconds.

Serve.

INGREDIENTS FOR 6 FISHERMEN

2 pounds sea scallops (large)
½ teaspoon sesame oil
½ teaspoon salt
1 large onion
pepper
2–3 tablespoons vegetable oil

COACH'S CORNER

- *When peeling onion, leave "bottom" intact. This will hold onion together while slicing. Remove bottom at the end of process and onion slices will separate easily.*
- *You can help the "softening" process by covering onions with a pot lid smaller than the pot or pan being used.*

degree of difficulty: 5

prep time: 10 minutes

cooking time: 15 minutes

INGREDIENTS
FOR 6 SWIMMERS

2 pounds sea scallops

salt and pepper

½ cup flour

1 stick butter

2 tablespoons vegetable oil

2 tablespoons garlic, chopped

2 tablespoons parsley, chopped

lemon wedges

COACH'S CORNER

● *Do not let the butter turn black. If it does, throw it out, clean the pan, and start over.*

■ *Do this procedure just before cooking the scallops.*

▲ *Keep the heat low so the garlic doesn't burn.*

SAUTÉED SCALLOPS WITH GARLIC AND PARSLEY

Jump in the pool with these deep-sea favorites. A perfect blend of scallops from the ocean and garlic from the fields of Provence. Often served in French restaurants as Scallops Provençal.

PLAYBOOK

● 1. Cook ½ of the butter and oil over medium-high heat until mixture sizzles.

2. Cook garlic until it becomes golden in color and remove to a side dish.

3. Using paper towels, pat scallops dry, and remove the small, hard muscle on the side.

4. Sprinkle with salt and pepper.

■ 5. Put flour and scallops in a paper or plastic bag and shake until scallops are coated with flour.

6. Discard excess flour.

7. Cook ½ of the scallops in butter/oil until golden brown (4–5 minutes). Continuously scrape bottom of pan as you cook, then remove scallops.

8. Add remaining butter to pan and cook balance of scallops as above.

▲ 9. Mix garlic and scallops over medium heat for 2 minutes.

10. Sprinkle with parsley.

Serve with quartered lemons.

STEAMED MUSSELS IN WHITE WINE AND HERBS

degree of difficulty: **4**
prep time: **15** minutes
cooking time: **10** minutes

An off-tackle slant scores every time and this recipe is a sure winner. A quick and delicious summer dish leaves plenty of time to enjoy the water.

PLAYBOOK

◆ 1. In a large pot, over medium-high heat, sauté the onions until they are softened.
2. Add the mussels, parsley, garlic, thyme, and pepper.
3. Pour in wine.
4. Bring the liquid to a boil over high heat.
5. Reduce the heat to medium-high and cook the mussels, covered, shaking the pan once or twice, for 5–6 minutes, or until the shells have opened.
6. *Discard any unopened mussels.*

Serve in soup bowls.

INGREDIENTS FOR 6 OFFENSIVE LINEMEN

● 4 pounds mussels, cleaned
1 cup chopped onion
½ stick butter (2 ounces)
3 tablespoons parsley, chopped
■ 1 tablespoon minced garlic
▲ 1 teaspoon fresh thyme, chopped
½ teaspoon pepper
2 cups dry white wine

COACH'S CORNER
● *Cleaned mussels available in super-market.*
■ *Chop fine or use a garlic press—do not use bottled or dried garlic.*
▲ *Use only ½ teaspoon if using dried thyme.*
◆ *Do not brown the onions.*

PASTA, RICE, AND POLENTA

Pasta Alfredo

Penne Toscano

Tagliatelle with Four Cheeses

Cold and Spicy Dan Dan Noodles

Spicy Rice with Peanuts
and Scallions

Grilled Polenta with Cheddar
or Jack Cheese

PASTA ALFREDO

degree of difficulty: 2
prep time: 10 minutes
cooking time: 2 minutes for
fresh pasta
12 minutes for
dried pasta

Climb the tallest mountain in Italy and you won't find a better recipe for this great classic dish. The options give the pasta an added flair.

PLAYBOOK

SAUCE

■ 1. Heat the cream, milk, and butter in a sauté pan.
2. Add ½ the cheese and a little freshly ground black pepper.
3. Whisk or stir with a fork, until smooth, then remove from the heat.

PASTA

1. Cook the fettuccine according to directions.
2. Remove pasta from water, discarding cooking water.
3. Add the cream sauce to the pasta.
4. Add the rest of the cheese, bacon, and peas.
5. Toss the noodles with the sauce.
6. Add black pepper.

Serve immediately.

INGREDIENTS
FOR 6–8 CLIMBERS

1 cup heavy cream
1 cup milk
3 tablespoons unsalted butter
1 cup freshly grated Parmesan cheese
● black pepper to taste
1 pound fettuccine or linguine
½ cup cooked peas (optional)
3 pieces cooked bacon, crumbled (optional)

COACH'S CORNER
● *Use pepper mill if available.*
■ *Do not boil!*

degree of difficulty: 2

prep time: 10 minutes

cooking time: 30 minutes

INGREDIENTS
FOR 4–6 ICE SKATERS

¼ cup extra virgin olive oil, plus
  3–4 tablespoons for the pasta
One 16-ounce can Italian plum
  tomatoes
1 pound penne
1 teaspoon salt
2 cloves garlic
6 ounces mozzarella cheese
1 teaspoon red pepper flakes,
  chopped (optional)

COACH'S CORNER

● *Water will boil faster
with the top on.*

■ *Pasta should be a little
"firm" to the bite. Do not
overcook.*

PENNE TOSCANO

A triple jump to the table when your guests
smell the aroma of Penne Toscano. This hollow
pasta allows the sauce to get inside as well as
outside. Always a favorite in Tuscany.

PLAYBOOK

PENNE

● 1. In a large, covered pot, bring 3 quarts water
     to a boil.
  2. Add the penne. When the water boils again, stir
     pasta with a long-handled spoon to separate.
■ 3. Follow the cooking instructions (less 30 sec-
     onds) on the package.
  4. Put pasta in a strainer and stir in 3–4 table-
     spoons olive oil.

SAUCE

  1. Chop the garlic fine or put it through a garlic
     press.
  2. Chop the mozzarella cheese into matchstick-
     sized shreds.
  3. Remove hard cores from the tomatoes.
     (Reserve all tomato liquids.)
  4. On medium-high setting, heat oil in a large
     pan. Add garlic, tomatoes, salt, red pepper
     flakes, and liquids and stir.
  5. Reduce heat to low and cook for 5 minutes.
  6. Add the cheese, stirring often for 2–3 minutes.
     When cheese has melted, the sauce is finished.
  7. Add the penne and stir over low heat, blend-
     ing the pasta and sauce together.

Serve in bowls heated in 150° oven for 10 minutes.

TAGLIATELLE WITH FOUR CHEESES

degree of difficulty: **3**
prep time: **10** minutes
cooking time: **15** minutes

After a day on the slopes, a heaping bowl of *quattro formaggio* is just the right ticket. With a piece of hearty Italian bread and a full-bodied wine, the meal is perfect.

PLAYBOOK

SAUCE (MAKE FIRST)

1. Pour the cream into a large saucepan and bring to a low boil over medium-high heat.
2. Slowly add the Swiss, Pecorino, and mozzarella cheeses, stirring to blend smoothly.
3. Add ½ the Parmesan, stirring to keep sauce smooth.
4. Continue to simmer over very low heat to melt cheeses completely.
5. When the mixture is smooth, taste it and, if needed, add salt and pepper.

PASTA (MAKE AFTER SAUCE IS DONE)

1. Bring a large pot of water to a boil.
2. When the water reaches a rolling boil, add the pasta.
■ 3. Cook 30 seconds less than called for in the package directions.
4. When the pasta is done, drain it very well and rinse briefly with cold water.
5. Pour the pasta into the saucepan with the cheese, mix, and reheat quickly if necessary.
▲ 6. Transfer the pasta to a warm serving bowl or individual plates and sprinkle the remaining Parmesan cheese over it.

Serve.

INGREDIENTS FOR 6 SKIERS

1 pound tagliatelle or tagliarini
● ¾ cup light cream
salt and black pepper

THE 4 CHEESES, ALL FRESH GRATED

⅓ cup Swiss (Emmental or Jarlsberg)
⅓ cup Pecorino
½ cup mozzarella
1 cup Parmesan cheese

COACH'S CORNER

● *Do not substitute milk or half-and-half: the sauce will not be thick enough.*
■ *Should be "firm" to the bite.*
▲ *Place bowl or plates in warm oven (150°) while preparing the pasta.*

degree of difficulty: 4

prep time: 15 minutes

cooking time: 12 minutes

INGREDIENTS
FOR 4–6 MIDFIELDERS

8 ounces spaghetti

1 tablespoon sesame seed oil

1 egg

1 tablespoon vegetable oil

2 slices baked ham, cut into
    thin strips

● 1 chicken breast, cooked and cut
    into strips

SAUCE

1 tablespoon chili sauce

¼ cup soy sauce

½ teaspoon salt

¼ cup red wine vinegar

COACH'S CORNER

● *Available in supermar-
ket or Chinese grocery
store.*

■ *Noodles should be
"firm" to the bite.*

COLD AND SPICY
DAN DAN NOODLES

A high, hard shot into the corner of the net. These zesty Chinese-style noodles are a perfect side dish with grilled chicken or fish. Can also be served as a light snack.

PLAYBOOK

1. *Preheat broiler for 15 minutes.*
2. Cook chicken under broiler for 4 minutes on each side, or until slightly brown.
3. Bring a large pot of water to a boil.
4. When the water reaches a rolling boil, add the pasta.
■ 5. Cook pasta 30 seconds less than called for in the package directions.
6. Rinse noodles with cold water right away. Drain.
7. Mix with sesame seed oil. Put pasta in refrigerator to chill.
8. Beat egg. Grease small skillet with 1 tablespoon oil.
9. Pour in egg and cook flat like an omelette.
10. Remove egg and cut into thin strips.
11. Arrange noodles on serving plate with ham, chicken, and egg on top.
12. Mix sauce ingredients in small bowl. Pour over covered noodles.

Serve cold.

SPICY RICE
WITH PEANUTS
AND SCALLIONS

You'll stop all shots with this sensational recipe from Asia. Full of rich flavors and textures, it's perfect with meat, fish, or chicken dishes. Your fans will cheer and shout!

PLAYBOOK

▲ 1. In a large pot, cook the garlic and the red pepper flakes in the oil over moderately low heat for 1 minute.
2. Add the rice.
3. Stir the mixture over moderate heat for 1 minute.
◆ 4. Add rice and water. Cover, and cook until the water is absorbed.
5. When rice is cooked, stir in salt, peanuts, scallions, and lime juice.

Serve immediately.

COACH'S CORNER
● *Crush between waxed paper or paper towel with the bottom of a frying pan.*
■ *Use 3–4 inch strips of both green and white parts, sliced thin.*
▲ *Be sure to select a pot that has a tight-fitting top. Rice directions will require a top.*
◆ *Cooking time will vary according to the type of rice. Follow directions on the rice package.*

---

degree of difficulty: 2
prep time: 10 minutes
cooking time: 20 minutes

INGREDIENTS
FOR 6–8 GOALIES

2 small garlic cloves, minced
½ teaspoon dried hot red pepper flakes
2 tablespoons vegetable oil
1 cup rice, uncooked
2 cups water
1 teaspoon salt
● ½ cup roasted peanuts, crushed
■ ½ cup scallions, thinly sliced
juice of 1 lime

GRILLED POLENTA WITH CHEDDAR OR JACK CHEESE

INGREDIENTS
FOR 6–8 BOXERS

- 1 cup polenta (yellow cornmeal)
  4 cans chicken broth
  1 tablespoon black pepper
  ½ stick butter (4 ounces)
  ½ pound Jack or Cheddar cheese, sliced

Deliver the knockout punch with a taste of Italian / American cooking. Long considered a staple in Italian home cooking, polenta is now featured in many fine restaurants.

COACH'S CORNER
- *Polenta can be served as an appetizer or as a vegetable.*

PLAYBOOK

1. In a large saucepan, bring broth and pepper to a boil.
2. Slowly add polenta, stirring with a whisk to avoid lumps.
3. Reduce heat to low and stir to prevent sticking.
4. Cook slowly for 10 minutes, stirring regularly.
5. Butter a large, shallow dish.
6. Pour in polenta to a depth of ½ inch, then smooth the top.
7. Set aside and let cool for 30 minutes.
8. *Preheat broiler for 15 minutes.*
9. Cut polenta into 4-inch squares.
10. Place squares on a cookie sheet or metal pan.
11. Grill until top surfaces are lightly toasted.
12. Turn, cover each with a slice of cheese, and grill until cheese melts.

Serve warm.

VEGETABLES

Snow Peas with Fresh Mushrooms

Baked Tomatoes with Herbs

Asparagus with Parmesan Cheese

Sesame Broccoli

Garlic String Beans

Carrots Gourmand

Potatoes with Italian Sausage

Baked Potatoes

Sautéed Mushrooms

SNOW PEAS WITH FRESH MUSHROOMS

degree of difficulty: 2
prep time: 3 minutes
cooking time: 8 minutes

Stretch the single into a double with this shot off the right-field wall. You only need a small portion to create an elegant and delicious side dish for any meal.

PLAYBOOK

1. Cut off hard ends of snow peas.
● 2. With damp cloth or paper towel, wipe off mushrooms and remove stems.
3. In a frying pan, heat 2 tablespoons of vegetable oil until very hot.
4. Put in snow peas. Stir-fry 3 minutes.
5. Remove peas, leaving hot oil in pan.
6. In same pan, sauté mushrooms for 3 minutes.
7. Add snow peas and broth.
8. Cook, over low heat, for 2 minutes.

Serve immediately.

COACH'S CORNER
● *Do not wash mushrooms.*

INGREDIENTS FOR 4–6 SLUGGERS

¼ pound snow peas, washed and dried
2 tablespoons vegetable oil
½ pound fresh mushrooms, sliced ⅛ inch thick
2 tablespoons chicken broth

degree of difficulty: 3
prep time: 15 minutes
cooking time: 15 minutes

INGREDIENTS
FOR 6 BATTERS

- 6 medium-sized tomatoes
- 3 large tomatoes
  salt and black pepper
  2 tablespoons olive oil
  4 garlic cloves, chopped
- ■ 1 teaspoon fresh tarragon, chopped
  2 tablespoons parsley, chopped
  2 tablespoons butter

COACH'S CORNER

- *Tomatoes should be ripe. If not, add 3 tablespoons tomato paste to chopped tomatoes.*
- ■ *If using dried tarragon, use ¹/₂ teaspoon, and rub the tarragon between your palms to release flavor.*

BAKED TOMATOES WITH HERBS

Your batting average will jump! Turn a simple tomato into a fine dining experience with this classic version of Tomatoes Provençal, heavily scented with the aromas of France.

PLAYBOOK

1. *Preheat oven to 400°.*
2. Cut the 3 large tomatoes in half.
3. Remove the seeds and water from inside the tomatoes.
4. Cut tomatoes into small pieces.
5. Heat the oil in a frying pan, add the cut tomatoes, salt, and pepper, and cook for 10 minutes, stirring occasionally.
6. Remove from the heat and add the garlic, tarragon, parsley, and butter.
7. Slice off the tops of the medium tomatoes.
8. Remove all of the seeds and water from the inside without damaging the pulp and skin.
9. Fill each tomato with the chopped tomato mixture.
10. Bake in oven for 12 minutes or until the tomatoes soften.

Serve.

ASPARAGUS WITH PARMESAN CHEESE

The perfect net game. Asparagus is now available year-round and makes a great partner with any main course. Can also be used as an appetizer with a hearty slice of Italian bread.

PLAYBOOK

1. Rinse asparagus under cold running water.
● 2. Fill a large pot halfway with water and bring to a boil.
3. Cook 5 minutes, until crisp but tender.
4. Remove from water and transfer to a serving dish.
5. Melt the butter in a small saucepan.
6. Drizzle butter over asparagus.
7. Sprinkle with salt, pepper, and Parmesan cheese.

Serve immediately.

COACH'S CORNER
● *For microwave: Put asparagus on plate, cover with plastic wrap, and cook on high for 2 minutes.*

degree of difficulty: 2
prep time: 2 minutes
cooking time: 6 minutes

INGREDIENTS FOR 6–8 TENNIS CHAMPS

1½ pounds asparagus
¾ cup Parmesan cheese, freshly grated
salt
freshly ground pepper
½ stick butter

degree of difficulty: 1
prep time: 5 minutes
cooking time: 3 minutes

INGREDIENTS
FOR 6 PITCHERS

1 large bunch broccoli
juice of 1 fresh lemon
1 tablespoon sesame seeds

SESAME BROCCOLI

A fast ball down the middle. This simple dish tastes good and is good for you.

PLAYBOOK

1. Rinse broccoli under cold running water.
2. Remove stems from broccoli about 1 inch below the green flowerets.
3. Put lemon juice in pot of boiling water (it keeps the broccoli green).
● 4. Boil broccoli 2–3 minutes, until tender.
■ 5. Sprinkle on sesame seeds.

Serve.

COACH'S CORNER
● *For microwave: Put broccoli on plate, cover with plastic wrap, and cook on high for 1–2 minutes. Drizzle with lemon and butter.*
■ *Broccoli can be adapted to any cuisine. Just add salsa for Tex-Mex, or olive oil for Italian.*

GARLIC STRING BEANS

degree of difficulty: 1
prep time: 5 minutes
cooking time: 6 minutes

A straight shot on goal. It just doesn't get any easier.

PLAYBOOK

- 1. Place string beans in boiling water for 3–5 minutes or microwave.
- 2. Remove while still crunchy.
- 3. While beans are cooking, melt butter in small saucepan over low heat and add garlic pieces for 1 minute.
- 4. Drizzle beans with garlic butter.

Serve immediately.

INGREDIENTS FOR 6 WINGERS

1 pound string beans
1 clove garlic, sliced thin
½ stick butter, melted

> ### COACH'S CORNER
> - *For microwave: Put beans on plate and cover with plastic wrap. Cook on high for 2 minutes.*

INGREDIENTS
FOR 6 REFEREES

2 pounds carrots, peeled and sliced

1 tablespoon vegetable or olive oil

½ cup onions, chopped

1 tablespoon fresh thyme, chopped

½ cup chicken broth

2 tablespoons maple syrup or
    honey

2 tablespoons parsley, chopped
    (optional)

CARROTS GOURMAND

How could you make that call? You won't dispute the referee on this decision. A healthy treat for everybody and a special favorite for the youngest rookies.

PLAYBOOK

1. Put the carrot slices in boiling water for 3 minutes.
2. In a frying pan, on medium-high, heat the oil.
3. Add the onions and, when translucent, add the thyme.
4. Reduce to medium-low and cook for 2 minutes.
5. Stir in the broth and maple syrup. Mix until smooth.
6. Add the cooked carrots.
7. Cover and continue cooking for 5 minutes.
8. Cook uncovered for 3 minutes to thicken the sauce.

Garnish with chopped parsley (optional) and serve.

COACH'S CORNER
● *Taste after 5 minutes to see if carrots are cooked to your taste.*

POTATOES WITH ITALIAN SAUSAGE

degree of difficulty: 2
prep time: 10 minutes
cooking time: 40 minutes

A powerful one-two punch to the midsection, with one of the great recipes to come out of southern Italy. You can get creative with many different herbs and spices: rosemary, thyme, or garlic.

PLAYBOOK

■ 1. Remove the skin from the sausage and break up the meat.

▲ 2. Heat the oil in a large frying pan or pot.

3. Add the meat, onion, and potatoes and cook, covered, over low heat for 30 minutes.

4. Uncover the pan and increase the heat to medium-high.

5. Sauté the potatoes until brown, stirring and scraping the bottom of the pan.

6. Salt and pepper to taste.

Serve.

INGREDIENTS FOR 6 WELTERWEIGHTS

● 3 large baking potatoes, peeled and sliced

½ pound Italian sausage, mild or spicy

3 tablespoons olive oil

salt and freshly ground pepper

1 onion, chopped

COACH'S CORNER

● *Russet or any brown-skinned potato.*

■ *Open the skin with a knife and remove the meat.*

▲ *Select a pan or pot with a cover.*

degree of difficulty: 1

prep time: 2 minutes

cooking time: 1 hour

INGREDIENTS FOR 6 WIDE RECEIVERS

- 6 medium baking potatoes
- 6 tablespoons butter *or*
    6 tablespoons mustard *or*
    6 tablespoons olive oil

salt and pepper

BAKED POTATOES

A first-round draft pick and the second half of the famous "meat and potatoes" team. This one needs no practice to be perfect.

PLAYBOOK

1. *Preheat oven to 425°.*
2. Wash potatoes under cold running water.
3. Prick each potato, in several places, with a knife.
4. Place potatoes on the wire oven rack in the middle of the oven.
5. Bake for 1 hour, turning on other side after 30 minutes.
6. Cut potatoes in half.
7. With fork, mash in one of the selected ingredients (butter, mustard, or olive oil).
▲ 8. Salt and pepper to taste.

COACH'S CORNER

- *Idaho or Russet potatoes preferred for baking.*
- *Butter is rich in taste, mustard is tangy, and olive oil is smooth.*
▲ *Do not add salt when using mustard.*

SAUTÉED MUSHROOMS

The cheering section will go wild with the robust taste of mushrooms. They can be eaten as a side vegetable, topped on salad or polenta, and even mashed into a baked potato.

PLAYBOOK

1. With a knife, cut and peel outer layers of onion.
- 2. Chop onion into small pieces.
  3. Heat oil over medium-high heat.
  4. Cook onions until they are translucent.
  5. Stir in sliced mushrooms and sauté (stir-fry) for 5 minutes or until soft.

Serve.

COACH'S CORNER
- *It is easier to cut an onion with the root end on. Remove when finished cutting.*

degree of difficulty: 1
prep time: 5 minutes
cooking time: 10 minutes

INGREDIENTS FOR 6–8 PLAYERS

2 tablespoons olive or vegetable oil
1 pound mushrooms, any variety
1 large or 2 medium onions

DESSERTS

Ice Cream Snowballs

Chunked Chocolate

Baked Apples

Apple-Berry Crisp

Fresh Strawberries Milanese

Caramelized Apple Slices
with Vanilla Ice Cream

Pear Purée with Fresh Strawberries

Peaches in Red Wine

Honey-Drizzled Fruit
with Ice Cream

Chocolate Ice Cream and
Mango Sorbet with Berries

Plain Chocolate Sauce

Chocolate Caramel Sauce

Orange Chocolate Sauce

ICE CREAM SNOWBALLS

You'll be first at the finish line with this easy recipe.

PLAYBOOK

1. Take ice cream out of freezer for ½ hour (to soften).
2. With two soup spoons, form ice cream balls—2 or 3 for each person.
3. Put ice cream in freezer to harden for 1 hour.
4. Roll ice cream in shredded coconut.
5. Pour chocolate sauce over ice cream and serve.

COACH'S CORNER

● *Premade ice cream balls can be purchased at ice cream stores.*

■ *See page 103 for recipe. Available at grocery or ice cream stores.*

---

degree of difficulty: **2**

prep time: **15** minutes

INGREDIENTS FOR 4–6 RUNNERS

● 1 pint vanilla ice cream
  1 package shredded coconut
■ 1 cup chocolate sauce

INGREDIENTS FOR 4–6 POINT GUARDS

- ½ pound block or piece of milk or semisweet chocolate (Belgian, Swiss, or other high quality)

CHUNKED CHOCOLATE

The perfect shot to end a big dinner. Simple and delicious.

PLAYBOOK

Using a large knife, cut chocolate into small pieces and put on plate.

Serve with coffee or tea.

COACH'S CORNER

- *Variation: Use ½ white and ½ brown chocolate.*

BAKED APPLES

degree of difficulty: 1

prep time: 5 minutes

cooking time: 60 minutes

One-half of America's most famous team, this is apple pie without the crust. A favorite since Grandma's days and still a perfect ending to the big game.

PLAYBOOK

1. *Preheat oven to 300°.*
2. Wash and dry the apples.
3. With a small knife, cut out 1½–2 inches of each core, starting at the top of the apple.
4. Fill each hole with 1 tablespoon sugar or honey.
5. Place the apples in an ovenproof baking dish and put on the middle shelf of the oven.
6. Cook for 60 minutes.
7. Remove and allow to cool.

● Serve warm or at room temperature.

COACH'S CORNER
● *Delicious with vanilla ice cream or raspberry sorbet.*

INGREDIENTS FOR 6 FORWARDS

6 apples, crisp and sharp (McIntosh or Fuji)
6 tablespoons sugar or honey

degree of difficulty: 3
prep time: 15 minutes
cooking time: 45 minutes

INGREDIENTS FOR 6 HALFBACKS

- 3 Granny Smith apples, peeled, cored, and sliced
  1 pint fresh or frozen blueberries, rinsed
  1 tablespoon fresh lemon juice
  ½ teaspoon cinnamon
  ½ stick butter
  ½ cup brown sugar
  ½ cup flour

APPLE-BERRY CRISP

Fourth and goal! This play guarantees a touchdown every time.

PLAYBOOK

1. *Preheat oven to 375°.*
2. Place apple slices in an ovenproof casserole or cake pan.
3. Sprinkle blueberries over apple slices.
4. Add lemon juice and cinnamon.
5. In a separate bowl, using a fork, blend the sugar, flour, and butter.
6. Spread mixture over the fruit.
7. Bake in oven for 45 minutes.

Serve.

COACH'S CORNER
- *The apples should be a little sour.*

FRESH STRAWBERRIES MILANESE

Take a perfect pass from the star forward and score the game-ending goal. This dessert packs punch in its perfect blend of balsamic vinegar and sugar to enhance the taste of the strawberries.

PLAYBOOK

1. Rinse strawberries under cold running water.
2. Slice berries in half.
3. Sprinkle with vinegar and sugar, then toss to blend.
4. Marinate, stirring occasionally, for 30 minutes.

Serve.

COACH'S CORNER
- *Use only balsamic vinegar.*

---

degree of difficulty: 2
prep time: 5 minutes
marinating time: 30 minutes

INGREDIENTS FOR 6 FORWARDS

2 pints strawberries, stems removed
- 6 tablespoons balsamic vinegar
3 tablespoons sugar

degree of difficulty: 3

prep time: 10 minutes

cooking time: 25 minutes

INGREDIENTS
FOR 6–8 JOCKEYS

4 large apples
- ½ stick butter

½ cup sugar

1 pint vanilla ice cream

CARAMELIZED APPLE SLICES WITH VANILLA ICE CREAM

We're off to the races with a dessert that's in the winner's circle every time. Easy and unique; sweet and tart. A refreshing idea for all seasons.

PLAYBOOK

1. Peel, remove core, and thinly slice the apples.
2. In a large frying pan, melt butter over medium-high heat.
- 3. Add apples in one layer and cook in the butter, turning once or twice, for 5 minutes.
4. Remove the slices as they brown.
5. Wipe pan clean.
6. Add sugar to pan.
7. Cook on high heat until sugar turns brown (5–7 minutes).
8. Add cooked apples and toss for 1 minute.

Serve warm or at room temperature, with ice cream.

COACH'S CORNER
- *Use only butter. Do not substitute.*
- *Cook in two batches.*

PEAR PURÉE WITH FRESH STRAWBERRIES

degree of difficulty: 3
prep time: 10 minutes
cooking time: 20 minutes

The perfect chip shot to end the meal.
Delightful when served with cake or ice cream.

PLAYBOOK

1. Chop pears.
2. Put chopped pears in a saucepan.
3. Add water, sugar, and lemon juice.
4. Cook, covered, over medium heat for
   20 minutes.
■ 5. Purée in a blender or food processor.
6. Pour over fresh strawberries.

Serve.

COACH'S CORNER

● *Pears must be ripe.*
■ *If equipment is unavailable, force pears
through a sieve with the back of a spoon.*

INGREDIENTS FOR 4–6 GOLFERS

● 3 large pears, skin and seeds
   removed
2 tablespoons water
¾ cup sugar
2 tablespoons lemon juice
2 pints fresh strawberries, washed

INGREDIENTS FOR
6 RACE DRIVERS

6 ripe peaches

6 teaspoons sugar

4 cups Chianti or other light,
    red wine

juice of ½ lemon

PEACHES IN RED WINE

This recipe picks up the checkered flag. A great recipe when the peaches are ripe and juicy.

PLAYBOOK

1. Halve the peaches and cut into slices.
2. Place the peach slices, unpeeled, in a deep bowl. Sprinkle with sugar.
3. Add lemon juice.
4. Add wine, then cover the bowl.
● 5. Let stand at room temperature for 4–5 hours or overnight.
6. Drain the sauce into a pan and boil until reduced by one-half.
7. Pour sauce over peaches.

Serve.

COACH'S CORNER
● *Do not refrigerate the peaches.*

HONEY-DRIZZLED FRUIT WITH ICE CREAM

A simple sprint to the finish line.

PLAYBOOK

- 1. Place two small scoops of ice cream on each plate or bowl.
  2. Wash and place berries around edge of ice cream.
  3. Pour honey into glass container.
- 4. Heat honey in microwave for 30 seconds.
  5. Drizzle honey on top of berries.

Serve immediately.

COACH'S CORNER
- *Best if served on cold plates.*
- *Can be done in small pot on top of stove using low heat.*

---

degree of difficulty: 1
prep time: 5 minutes
cooking time: 30 seconds

INGREDIENTS FOR 4–6 RELAY RUNNERS

1 pint (small carton) fresh berries
1 pint ice cream
½ cup honey

degree of difficulty: 1

prep time: 20 minutes

INGREDIENTS FOR
8–10 CLEAN-UP BATTERS

1 pint chocolate ice cream

1 pint mango or orange sorbet

• 1 pint raspberries or strawberries

CHOCOLATE ICE CREAM AND MANGO SORBET WITH BERRIES

A game-ending blast into the stands.

PLAYBOOK

1. Take ice cream and sorbet out of the freezer 15 minutes before serving.
2. On the kitchen counter, put out 1 soup bowl or other shallow dish for each person.
3. Using a soup spoon, place two spoonfuls of ice cream *and* sorbet on each dish.
4. Rinse fresh berries under cold running water.
5. Sprinkle berries on each plate.

Serve.

COACH'S CORNER
• *Berries can be either fresh or frozen.*

PLAIN CHOCOLATE SAUCE

degree of difficulty: 1
prep time: 5 minutes
cooking time: 2 minutes

An easy recipe for soccer moms.

PLAYBOOK

1. Chop candy bar into small pieces.
2. Put in small glass bowl.
3. Add water.
■ 4. Cook in microwave for 1 minute.
5. Blend with fork until smooth.
6. Add crushed nuts, if desired.
7. Allow to cool for 15 minutes.

INGREDIENTS FOR 4–6 SOCCER PLAYERS

3½-ounce milk chocolate bar
4 tablespoons water
● ½ cup crushed cashews or peanuts (optional)

COACH'S CORNER
● *Can be crushed in waxed paper or paper towel with bottom of frying pan or pot.*
■ *Can be heated in small saucepan. Do not boil.*

INGREDIENTS FOR 4–6 SQUAD MEMBERS

3½-ounce chocolate caramel candy bar

4 tablespoons water

CHOCOLATE CARAMEL SAUCE

Another easy recipe for players and coaches.

PLAYBOOK

1. Chop candy bar into small pieces.
2. Put in small glass bowl.
- 3. Cook in microwave for 1 minute.
4. Remove and, with fork, blend in water.
5. Cook another 1 minute in microwave.
6. Remove and blend until smooth.
7. Allow to cool for 15 minutes.

COACH'S CORNER
- *Can be done in small pot on top of stove using low heat.*

ORANGE CHOCOLATE SAUCE

This combination of orange and chocolate is a favorite among downhill racers because of its sophisticated contrast of flavors.

PLAYBOOK

1. Break or cut chocolate bar into pieces.
2. Place in glass bowl and add juice.
- 3. Microwave on high for 30 seconds.
4. Remove and stir with fork.
5. Allow to cool for 15 minutes.
6. Add liqueur (optional).

Serve over ice cream or fruit.

COACH'S CORNER
- *Can be done in small pot on top of stove using low heat.*

degree of difficulty: 1
prep time: 5 minutes
cooking time: 2 minutes

INGREDIENTS FOR 4–6 SKIERS

3 ounces high-quality semisweet or bittersweet chocolate
1 teaspoon sugar
3 tablespoons orange juice
2 ounces Grand Marnier or other orange-flavored liqueur (optional)

PREP, COOKING TIME, AND UTENSILS

	prep time (minutes)	cooking time (minutes)	equipment list
APPETIZERS			
Melon and Parma Ham	5	0	knife
Smoked Salmon with Honey Mustard Sauce	10	0	knife, spoon
Carpaccio	5	0	knife
Shrimp Cocktail	15	7–8	pot, knife
Spareribs	15	60	dish, pan, knife
Cheese Toasts with Basil and Sun-Dried Tomatoes	10	4–7	knife, baking sheet
Bruschetta: Garlic Toasts with Tomatoes and Basil	5	2	knife, fork
SOUPS			
Gazpacho	15	5	pot, blender, knife
Onion Soup	10	50	knife, soup pot
Onion and Tomato Soup	10	135	knife, pot, blender, pan
Crabmeat and Asparagus Soup	4	10	knife, pot, fork
Pasta and Bean Soup	15	40	pot, knife, blender
Corn and Shrimp Chowder	15	15	knife, blender, pot
VEGETABLE SALADS			
Mozzarella, Tomatoes, and Basil	5	0	knife
Tomato and Basil Salad with Goat Cheese	10	0	knife

	prep time (minutes)	cooking time (minutes)	equipment list
Blue Cheese Salad	30	0	knife
Caesar Salad with Grilled Chicken	15	15	broiling pan, knife, fork
Green Beans and Mushrooms with Walnut Dressing	10	2	pot, knife, blender, fork
Green Salad with Parmesan Cheese Chips	5	10	knife, spatula, fork, oven pan

SEAFOOD SALADS

Shrimp and Potato Salad	15	25	knife, bowl, fork
Curried Seafood Salad	30	30	pot, knife, bowls (2)
Pasta Salad with Shrimp and Pine Nuts	15	20	pot, knife, pan, bowls (2), whisk
Shrimp and Crabmeat Salad	20	20	bowl, pot, knife
Salade Niçoise	20	15	bowl, pot, fork, knife

CHICKEN

French Roasted Chicken with Herbs de Provence	10	70–80	cup, ovenproof dish, knife, fork
Roasted Chicken in White Wine	20	45	bowl, pan, plastic bag, spoon
Grilled Chicken Italiano	15	10–12	waxed paper, frying pan, spatula, fork, broiling pan
Country-Style Chicken	20	50	ovenproof pot, knife, spoon
Honey Chicken	5	40	knife, large pan, fork, cup
Sautéed Chicken in Mustard Sauce	10	25	frying pan, spatula, knife, platter, spoon

	prep time (minutes)	cooking time (minutes)	equipment list
BEEF AND VEAL			
Pepper Steak	10	10	frying pan, spatula, fork
Beef with Scallions	10	5	frying pan, spatula, fork, cup
Veal Marsala	15	15	waxed paper, frying pan, spatula, spoon
Veal Chops with Garlic and Rosemary	10	15	bowl, fork, knife, broiler pan
Ground Steak with Blue Cheese and Green Peppercorn Sauce	10	20	bowl, knife, fork, frying pan, spatula, spoon, whisk
Pan-Seared Veal Chops with Brandy Mustard Sauce	10	30	knife, fork, frying pan, spatula, ovenproof dish
FISH			
Grilled Salmon with Mustard and Tarragon	15	5–10	bowl, fork, glass dish, broiling pan
Broiled Rockfish with Fennel and Walnut Oil	3	15–20	cup, grilling pan
Grilled Swordfish with Capers, Lemon, and Garlic	10	8–10	spoon, fork, knife, broiling pan
Tuna Wrapped in Bacon	5	8	knife, spoon, toothpicks
Grilled Swordfish with Salsa	10	8	knife, tablespoon, broiling pan
Steamed Rockfish or Sea Bass with Black Beans	10	30	knife, teaspoon, ovenproof dish, aluminum foil

	prep time (minutes)	cooking time (minutes)	equipment list
SHELLFISH			
Crispy Shrimp Wrapped in Bacon	10	12	knife, bowl, toothpicks, frying pan, fork
Shrimp with Olive Oil and Lemon	10	15	pot, knife
Lobster Medallions with Chive Sauce	10	10	knife, cup, plastic wrap, frying pan, spatula, fork, spoon
Maryland Crab Cakes	15	25	knife, frying pan, spatula, bowl, ovenproof dish
Stir-Fried Scallops with Onions	15	15	knife, frying pan, fork or long spoon
Sautéed Scallops with Garlic and Parsley	10	15	frying pan, knife, plastic bag, spatula
Steamed Mussels in White Wine and Herbs	15	10	knife, pot, large spoon
PASTA, RICE, AND POLENTA			
Pasta Alfredo	10	2–12	small pot, large pot, fork, strainer (optional)
Penne Toscano	10	30	knife, large pot, strainer, pan, fork
Tagliatelle with Four Cheeses	10	15	saucepan, fork, large pot, strainer
Cold and Spicy Dan Dan Noodles	15	12	oven pan, large pot, strainer, frying pan, knife, bowl
Spicy Rice with Peanuts and Scallions	10	20	knife, cup, large pot with top
Grilled Polenta with Cheddar or Jack Cheese	45	10	knife, saucepan, fork or whisk, shallow dish, oven pan

	prep time (minutes)	cooking time (minutes)	equipment list
VEGETABLES			
Snow Peas with Fresh Mushrooms	3	8	knife, spoon, frying pan, fork or spatula
Baked Tomatoes with Herbs	15	15	knife, spoon, frying pan, oven-proof dish
Asparagus with Parmesan Cheese	2	6	large pot, fork, saucepan
Sesame Broccoli	5	3	knife, pot
Garlic String Beans	5	6	knife, pot
Carrots Gourmand	10	20	knife, pot, frying pan, fork
Potatoes with Italian Sausage	10	40	knife, large pan with cover, spatula
Baked Potatoes	2	60	knife, fork
Sautéed Mushrooms	5	10	knife, frying pan, fork or spatula
DESSERTS			
Icd Cream Snowballs	15	0	2 soup spoons
Chunked Chocolate	1	0	knife
Baked Apples	5	60	small knife, plastic wrap
Apple-Berry Crisp	15	45	knife, ovenproof dish, bowl, fork
Fresh Strawberries Milanese	5	30	bowl, spoon
Caramelized Apple Slices with Vanilla Ice Cream	10	25	knife, frying pan
Pear Purée with Fresh Strawberries	10	20	knife, saucepan, blender or food processor
Peaches in Red Wine	15	4–5 hours	knife, bowl
Honey-Drizzled Fruit with Ice Cream	5	$\frac{1}{2}$	spoon, bowl

	prep time (minutes)	cooking time (minutes)	equipment list
Chocolate Ice Cream and Mango Sorbet with Berries	20	0	2 soup spoons
Plain Chocolate Sauce	5	2	knife, bowl, fork
Chocolate Caramel Sauce	3	2	knife, bowl, fork
Orange Chocolate Sauce	5	2	knife, bowl, fork

GLOSSARY

Adjust for seasoning
With a fork or spoon, take a little taste of what you are cooking. Add a little salt and pepper if it needs it, or maybe a little garlic or herbs to enhance the flavor.

Baking sheet
A metal tray that slides into the oven. Often used for baking cookies. It is a versatile kitchen tool.

Beat slightly
To use a fork to blend elements, such as white and yolk of an egg.

Blend
To mix together two or more ingredients.

Blender
A machine with small blades that blends materials together. Do not use it to whip potatoes.

Blend with fork
To use a fork to do the mixing. Usually provides a lighter blending.

Boil
To bring liquid to a point where bubbles break the flat surface; it is often the desired cooking point.

Broil
To cook with direct heat from either above (oven broiler) or below (charcoal, gas, or wood-burning grill).

Broiler
The heating element inside the oven.

Buttered sheet
A flat metal sheet (one that fits into the oven when the door is closed) and is spread with a light coating of butter or cooking spray before being used.

Cheese rind
The skin of the cheese; it can be very hard or soft.

Cheese shaver
A bladed kitchen instrument that cuts cheese into thin layers. Does not work on soft cheeses.

Chicken—skinless-boneless
Refers to chicken breasts that have had the skin and bones removed. Can be purchased in this manner and provides an easy method for preparing many chicken dishes.

Chill
To place a food or kitchen implement in the refrigerator (or freezer) prior to use.

Chop
To use a heavy knife and cut into small, bite-sized pieces. See "Mince."

Chop coarsely
To chop, as above, but into uneven pieces.

Coat
To cover evenly.

Cold plates
Plates that have been refrigerated prior to use. For example, a cold plate will

preserve the freshness of a salad, or will prevent ice cream from melting too quickly.

Core

To cut out the middle, or inedible portion, often including the seeds or fibrous stalk.

Cover

Covering a pot hastens the cooking process by trapping the steam inside the pot. When boiling water, you can reduce the boiling time by $\frac{1}{2}$ when the pot is covered. Often used for slow-cooking foods, since you can use a low heat and not toughen the cooked product.

Crisp apple

An apple that is hard to the bite, or crunchy.

Crumble

To break into small pieces.

Crumbled—bacon

Bacon that is first cooked crispy, blotted with paper towels to remove cooking fat, and then broken into small pieces.

Crushed garlic

Garlic that is mashed through a garlic press. If press is not available, it may be crushed by sprinkling with a little salt and then mashing with the back of a spoon or knife.

Deep-fry

To immerse in boiling cooking oil or fat.

Deglaze

To remove small particles of food left on the bottom of the pan or pot as a result of

the cooking process. Procedure: add vinegar or wine to the pan, raise the temperature very high, and scrape the pieces off the bottom of the pan with a long-handled spoon or spatula.

Devein

To remove the black or pink vein from the back of the shrimp. With a sharp knife, cut a small slice down the back, and then spread the shrimp apart. Remove the vein with your fingers while washing under cold running water.

Done, when done

The most difficult task for a cook, especially the rookie. Cut off a small piece and taste to see if cooked. Or, cook an extra piece and cut open to see if it is cooked properly.

Drain

To remove cooking fat or water, use a strainer, or use the pot lid and allow a slight crack for the water to run through. If liquid is cool enough, you can put a slightly smaller plate on top and tilt bowl or pot and allow excess to run off.

Dried herbs

Dried herbs are much stronger and more concentrated than fresh herbs. To release the flavor of dried herbs, you must rub them in the palm of your hand before using.

Drizzle

To sprinkle. Place a small amount in a cup and either 1) pour in a thin stream, or 2) using the prongs of a fork, dip into the cup and drop in a little at a time.

Extra virgin olive oil
The oil made from the first pressing of the olives. The label will read "extra virgin."

Food mill / Food processor
An electric or hand-powered device used to grind or mix food.

Fresh grated cheese
Cheeses used in cooking should be freshly grated and not stored on the shelf in a bottle.

Fry
To cook in hot oil or fat. See "Stir-fry."

Garlic press
See "Crushed garlic."

Grease a baking or cookie sheet
To coat an ovenproof dish or pan with butter or oil to prevent sticking and to allow easy removal of food after cooking.

Grilling tray
A tray that slides into grooves at the adjustable sides of the oven to allow grilling at varying distances from the heating element.

Halve
To cut in half.

Hard-boiled eggs
Using a spoon, lower uncooked eggs into boiling water for 14 minutes. Remove and immediately place in cold water to stop cooking process. To remove shell, roll on hard surface (sink or counter) and crush slightly to crack.

Heavy pan
A flat or frying pan with a heavy bottom that allows heat to be distributed more evenly.

Hot plates
Place empty dinner plates in oven for 10 minutes at 150°. Allows a hot meal to remain warm for up to 30 minutes. Remove from oven with dishtowel or oven glove.

Line a pan
To cover the bottom of grilling or cooking pan with tin foil. Substantially reduces cleanup.

Log of chèvre
Many goat cheeses (French word for goat is *chèvre*) are sold in the shape of a log.

Long-handled spoon
Good for stirring hot, stovetop recipes.

Marinade
A combination of herbs, spices, and liquids into which food is placed to absorb the flavors. In some instances, the marinade will cook the food.

Marinate
The act of placing the food in the marinade.

Mash in
To combine, usually with a fork.

Measuring cup/drinking glass
Measuring devices are useful in the kitchen but not essential. A large drinking glass contains 8 ounces of liquid, or 1 cup. Therefore, you can judge ¼ cup or ½ cup by using a drinking glass.

Mince

To chop finely with the blade of a knife.

Ovenproof

A glass or metal dish that will go in the oven and will not break in the cooking process. CAUTION: an ordinary ceramic dinner plate can withstand temperatures of 500° but will crack under the heat of a high broiler.

Pan-fry

To fry in a pan using less oil or butter so the food is not submerged in cooking liquid.

Pat dry

To remove excess fat or liquid by drying on paper towels, napkins, or dishtowels.

Peel

To remove the outer skin. Applies to certain fruits, vegetables, seafood, etc.

Peel—shrimp

To remove the head, tail, and shell, leaving nothing but the meat. Shrimp can be peeled before or after cooking.

Pepper mill

A device used for grinding black pepper. Freshly ground pepper is desirable for many dishes.

Plunge

To immerse in cold water. It is a necessary step in stopping the cooking process for some dishes.

Potato peeler / vegetable peeler

A useful kitchen device that contains a small blade used for removing the skin from potatoes and other vegetables such as carrots and asparagus. Peeling is often unnecessary, though, if food is washed thoroughly.

Preheated broiler

See below.

Preheated oven

An oven that is heated prior to putting in food. Most food should be prepared in a preheated oven.

Purée

To make into a soft paste or liquid, usually with a blender or food processor.

Quarter

To cut in four parts. With fowl (chicken, duck, turkey, etc.), it means to remove the legs and wings and cut the breast in half.

Red pepper—hot

Generally refers to flakes of chili peppers. Found in the spice section of the store.

Red pepper—sweet

Generally refers to bell peppers, which are grown red, green, and yellow. Available in the vegetable section of the grocery store.

Roast

To cook uncovered in the oven.

Rolling boil

The stage when water is boiling violently.

Rub

To cover food, by applying with the fingers, a layer of herbs and spices.

Sauté

To cook quickly, in a frying pan, with a small amount of oil. Can eliminate or substantially reduce oil in a nonstick pan.

Scrape bottom of pan

With spatula, to remove small food particles often stuck to the bottom of the cooking surface. These particles can be important to the flavor of sauces.

Shrimp size

Generally determined by number of uncooked shrimp in a pound: jumbo (10–15), extra large (16–20), large (21–30), medium (31–35), and small (36–45).

Simmer

To cook a liquid at a temperature just below the boiling point, when bubbles barely break the surface.

Sizzle

The sound of butter, oil, or other fat when it is ready for cooking.

Spatula

A flat-bladed cooking implement used for lifting or scraping.

Stir

To mix by turning or folding.

Stir-fry

To cook small portions of food by briskly turning in cooking liquid or in a non-stick pan.

Strainer

A kitchen utensil with holes or mesh in the bottom that allows for the removal of cooking water while leaving the food in the strainer

Tablespoon

A measurement equal to 3 teaspoons.

Teaspoon

A measurement equal to $\frac{1}{3}$ tablespoon.

Toast

The process of browning or crisping in a toaster, under the broiler, or on top of a grill.

Tomato Paste

A thick, tomato purée. Can be purchased in a can or tube.

Toss

To mix gently, with forks or fingers.

To taste

To season to an individual's taste. After tasting, you may find the dish requires more salt, pepper, herbs, or spices.

Vinaigrette

A salad dressing or marinade with a base of 3 parts vinegar to 1 part oil.

Warm plates

See "Hot plates."

Whisk

A kitchen utensil made of wire loops used to lighten by beating air into the product. Very often a fork may be used to whisk ingredients together.

WINE

PERFECT PLAYMATES

MAJOR LEAGUE SELECTIONS, $10–$20

APPETIZERS AND SALADS

Any white wine listed below for chicken, fish, or shellfish. Wine is *not* served with *vinegar dressing* because the acid in the vinegar destroys the flavor of the wine.

CHICKEN

Vendange—Merlot (red) Fruity and smooth. The perfect pitch. Under $10.

Columbia Crest—Chardonnay (white) Apple-like flavor makes the highlights. Under $10.

Dunnigan Hills Barrel Cuvée—Chardonnay (white) A sure par on the 18th. The right shot. Under $12.

Cambria—Chardonnay (white) A clean, crisp wine. A slam dunk. Under $12.

Kendall-Jackson Paradise Valley—Chardonnay (white) A wine soaked in the flavors of peach, pears, and honey. Just the ticket. Under $20.

FISH

Nobilo—Sauvignon Blanc (white) As good as a seat on the 50-yard line. A fresh and lively wine. Under $12.

Koonunga Hills—Shiraz Cabernet (red) This smooth, plush wine adds zest to all seafood. Under $12.

COACH'S CORNER

WHITE WINE

1. *Serve chilled (refrigerate 1–1½ hours before serving).*
2. *Fill the glass about ⅔ full.*
3. *There are approximately 8 servings per bottle.*
4. *White wine is best served with fish and chicken.*

RED WINE

1. *Generally serve at dining room temperature.*
2. *Place bottle in dining room 2–3 hours before serving.*
3. *Open 1 hour before serving.*
4. *Fill the glass about ½ full.*
5. *You will get about 10 servings per bottle.*
6. *Red wine is best served with meat and chicken.*

Cuvée Angeline—Sauvignon Blanc (white) You'll circle the bases with this refreshing and elegant wine. Under $12.

Kunde—Sauvignon Blanc (white) The perfect selection for players and spectators. Under $15.

SHELLFISH

Les Jamelles—Chardonnay (white) An easy play every time. Both fruity and spicy. Under $10.

Château Ste. Michelle—Chardonnay (white) Never a reverse with this lush, full-bodied wine. Under $14.

McGuigan—Shiraz (red) A bright and fruity wine from Australia that improves throughout the meal. Under $14.

Benzinger—Merlot (red) Superb, intense wine from California. A first-round pick with any red sauce. Under $12.

Turning Leaf—Chardonnay (white) A smooth, rich, and exciting touchdown. Under $12.

PASTA, RICE, AND POLENTA

Banfi Vintner's Toscana "Col di Sasso" (red) The beautiful Tuscan wine brings out the full flavor of your pasta. Under $10.

Kendall-Jackson Vintner's Reserve—Pinot Noir (red) The perfect lineup for any rich pasta dinner. Under $15.

Hardy's—Merlot (red) Bring the crowd to its feet with this smooth, deep wine with rich berry flavors. Under $20.

Cousino-Macul—Merlot (red) The Chileans have produced a great player with this excellent, full-bodied wine. A great choice. Under $15.

BEEF AND VEAL

Hardy's Notting Hill—Merlot (red) This medium-bodied wine is a sure shot. Excellent smell and taste. Goes well with cheese and spicy sausage. Under $10.

Georges Duboeuf—Beaujolais (red) Put this wine on-the-line when you put beef on the table. Light, fruity, and spicy. Under $11.

Cline Cellars—California Zinfandel (red) Whether with grilled hot dogs or hamburgers, this full-bodied selection brings out the great flavors. Under $11.

Vinha Do Monte Alentejo—(red) Surprise the crowd with this end run from Portugal. Powerful and deep, but with a soft elegance that will please everyone. Under $12.

Clos du Bois—Merlot (red) A luscious wine with superb bench strength. A powerful choice of toasted oak and cherries. Under $20.

INDEX

chèvre. *See* goat cheese

chicken, 37–44; country-style, 42; in dan-dan noodles, 76; French roasted with herbs de Provence, 39; grilled, Italiano, 41; grilled, with Caesar salad, 26; honey, 43; roasted in white wine, 40; sautéed in mustard sauce, 44; skinless-boneless, definition of, 113; wines for, 119

chicken broth: in baked carrots, 86; in beef with scallions, 48; in brandy mustard sauce, 52; in corn and shrimp chowder, 20; in country-style chicken, 42; in crabmeat and asparagus soup, 18; in grilled polenta with cheddar/jack cheese, 78; in onion soup, 16; in snow peas with fresh mushrooms, 81

chill, definition of, 113

chive sauce, lobster medallions with, 65

chocolate, chunked, 94

chocolate ice cream, and mango sorbet with berries, 102

chocolate sauce, 103; caramel, 104; with ice cream snowballs, 93; orange, 105

chop, definition of, 113

chop coarsely, definition of, 113

chunked chocolate, 94

clam juice, in lobster medallions with chive sauce, 65

Cline Cellars California Zinfandel, 120

Clos du Bois Merlot, 120

coat, definition of, 113

cocktail sauce, 8

coconut, in ice cream snowballs, 93

cold plates, definition of, 113–14

Columbia Crest Chardonnay, 119

cooking times, 107–11

core, definition of, 114

corn and shrimp chowder, 20

Cousino-Macul Merlot, 120

cover, definition of, 114

crab cakes, Maryland, 66

crabmeat: in crabmeat and asparagus soup, 18; in curried seafood salad, 32; in shrimp and crabmeat salad, 34

cream: in chicken sautéed in mustard sauce, 44; in ground steak with blue cheese and green

peppercorn sauce, 51; in pasta Alfredo, 73; in tagliatelle with four cheeses, 75

crisp apple, definition of, 114

crumble, definition of, 114

curried seafood salad, 32

Cuvée Angeline Sauvignon Blanc, 120

dan-dan noodles, 76

deep-fry, definition of, 114

deglaze, definition of, 114

desserts, 91–105; apple-berry crisp, 96; baked apples, 95; caramelized apple slices with vanilla ice cream, 98; chocolate ice cream and mango sorbet with berries, 102; chunked chocolate, 94; honey-drizzled fruit with ice cream, 101; ice cream snowballs, 93; peaches in red wine, 100; pear purée with fresh strawberries, 99; strawberries Milanese, 97

devein, definition of, 114

done, definition of, 114

drain, definition of, 114

dried herbs, definition of, 114

drizzle, definition of, 114

Dunnigan Hills Barrel Cuvée Chardonnay, 119

eggs: in crabmeat and asparagus soup, 18; in crispy shrimp wrapped in bacon, 63; in ground steak with blue cheese and green peppercorn sauce, 51; hard-boiled, definition of, 115; in Maryland crab cakes, 66; in salade niçoise, 35

Emmental cheese, in tagliatelle with four cheeses, 75

extra virgin olive oil, definition of, 115

fennel, broiled rockfish with, 56

fettuccine, in pasta Alfredo, 73

fish, 53–60; broiled rockfish with fennel and walnut oil, 56; grilled salmon with mustard and tarragon, 55; grilled swordfish with capers, lemon, and garlic, 57; grilled swordfish with salsa, 59; steamed rockfish/sea bass with black beans, 60; tuna wrapped in bacon, 58; wines for, 119–20. *See also* seafood salads

food mill/processor, definition of, 115

French bread: in Caesar salad, 26; in onion soup, 16; in tomato and basil salad with goat cheese, 24

fruit, honey-drizzled, with ice cream, 101

fry, definition of, 115

garlic: crushed, definition of, 114; grilled swordfish with, 57; and rosemary, veal chops with, 50; sautéed scallops with, 68; with string beans, 85; toasts, with tomatoes and basil, 11

gazpacho, 15

Georges Duboeuf Beaujolais, 120

ginger: in honey chicken, 43; with steamed rockfish/sea bass, 60

goat cheese, 115; in cheese toasts, 10; with tomato and basil salad, 24

Grand Marnier, in orange chocolate sauce, 105

grease baking/cookie sheet, definition of, 115

green beans: and mushrooms with walnut dressing, 27; in salade niçoise, 35

green peppercorn sauce, and blue cheese, ground steak with, 51

green salad with Parmesan cheese chips, 28

grilling tray, definition of, 115

halve, definition of, 115

ham: in dan-dan noodles, 76; Parma, and melon, 5; with steamed rockfish/sea bass, 60

hard-boiled eggs, definition of, 115

Hardy's Merlots, 120

heavy pan, definition of, 114

herbs: baked tomatoes with, 82; de Provence, French roasted chicken with, 39; dried, definition of, 115; steamed mussels in white wine with, 69

hoisin sauce, with spareribs, 9

honey: in baked apples, 95; in carrots gourmand, 86; drizzled on fruit with ice cream, 101

honey mustard sauce, smoked salmon with, 6

hot plates, definition of, 115

ice cream: with caramelized apple slices, 98; with honey-drizzled fruit, 101; and mango sorbet with berries, 102; snowballs, 93

Italian sausage, potatoes with, 87

jack cheese, grilled polenta with, 78

Jarlsberg cheese, in tagliatelle with four cheeses, 75

Kendall-Jackson: Paradise Valley Chardonnay, 119; Vintner's Reserve Pinot Noir, 120

Koonunga Hills Shiraz Cabernet, 119

Kunde Sauvignon Blanc, 120

lemon: grilled swordfish with, 57; and olive oil, shrimp with, 64

Les Jamelles Chardonnay, 120

lettuce: Boston, in salade niçoise, 35; in shrimp and crabmeat salad, 34; in shrimp and potato salad, 31. See also Romaine lettuce

line pan, definition of, 115

linguine, in pasta Alfredo, 73

lobster medallions, with chive sauce, 65

log of goat cheese, definition of, 115

long-handled spoon, definition of, 115

mango: chutney, with curried seafood salad, 32; sorbet, and chocolate ice cream with berries, 102

maple syrup, in carrots gourmand, 86

marinade, definition of, 115

marinate, definition of, 115

Marsala wine, veal with, 49

Maryland crab cakes, 66

mash in, definition of, 115

McGuigan Shiraz, 120

measuring cup, definition of, 114

melon, and Parma ham, 5

menus, viii

mesclun, in green salad with Parmesan cheese chips, 28

mince, definition of, 116

mozzarella cheese: in penne Toscano, 74; salad with tomatoes and basil, 23; in tagliatelle with four cheeses, 75

mushrooms: in brandy mustard sauce, 52; with chicken roasted in white wine, 40; and green beans with walnut dressing, 27; sautéed, 89; snow peas with, 81

mussels, steamed, in white wine with herbs, 69

ABOUT THE AUTHOR

PAUL B. ABRAMS began his career as an amateur baseball player and an acclaimed sportswriter. He wrote for the Hearst newspaper syndicate before going on to develop a successful chain of retail food and catering businesses in Washington, D.C. He has written numerous articles and short stories about his food experiences.

Paul has remained an ardent sports fan while developing a keen interest in the methods and components of good food preparation. He has traveled extensively throughout the United States, Europe, and Asia and has furthered his skills with studies in London at Cordon Bleu Cooking School and Prudence Leith Cookery School; in France at the Michelin-starred restaurant Le Moulin des Mougins; in Italy with Marcella Hazan at the Hotel Cipriani in Venice; and in Washington, D.C., at L'Académie de Cuisine.

In this gourmet guide for rookies, he combines all his passions—sports, writing, travel, and cooking. *The Sport of Cooking* translates the natural instincts associated with sports into basic kitchen skills to help the rookie chef produce delicious gourmet meals, quickly and efficiently—just like an old pro.